Kariakor

The Carrier Corps

The War Memorial, Kenyatta Avenue, Nairobi. From left: Carrier, King's African Rifleman, Arab Rifleman

Inscription

SWAHILI

Haya ni makumbusho ya askari
wa nti za huko Africa
waliopigana katika vita
pamoja na watukuzi
waliokuwa ni miguu
na mikono ya hao askari
na watu wote wengine
waliotumika wakafa
kwa ajili ya Mfalme wao
na nti za mshariki ya Afrika
katika vita vikubwa 1914-1918.
  *Mutakapo pigana kwa nti zenu
  hatta mukifa vijana vyenu
  watakumbuka majina yenu.*

ENGLISH

This is to the memory of the
native African troops who
fought, to the Carriers who
were the feet and hands of
the army, and to all other
men who served and died
for their King and country
in Eastern Africa in the Great
War, 1914-1918.
  *If you fight for your country
  even if you die, your sons
  will remember your name.*

Kariakor

The Carrier Corps

The Story of the Military Labour Forces
in the Conquest of German East Africa, 1914 to 1918

GEOFFREY HODGES

Abridged Edition
Edited by ROY GRIFFIN

Nairobi University Press

First Published 1999 by
Nairobi University Press
University of Nairobi
P.O. Box 30197
Nairobi

© Geoffrey Hodges

University of Nairobi Library CIP Data
　　Hodges, Geoffrey
　　　　Kariakor: the story of the military labour forces in the conquest of German East Africa, 1914 to 1918/G. Hodges.-abridged edition.- Nairobi: Nairobi University Press, 1999.
　　247 pp.
　　1. World War, 1914-1918 -- campaigns -- Africa, East.   1 Title
　　D 547.A2H6

ISBN 9966 846 44 1

Printed by **Downtown Printing Works Ltd.**
P O Box 75207 •Tel 253342, Nairobi

In memory of the carriers who were the feet and hands of the army

Table of Contents

Dedication	v
List of Plates	ix
List of Tables and Maps	x
Preface to the Abridged Edition	xi
Acknowledgments	xiii

Introduction - The Carrier Corps in History 1

Chapter One - African Labour

Labour Before the War	4
The Carrier Corps	13

Chapter Two - The War Strategy

British Imperial Strategy	23
Recruiting in East Africa Protectorate	33
Carrier Logistics	47

Chapter Three - In the Battlefields

Defending the Uganda Railway: 1914-15	58
Preparing to Attack: 1915-16	69
The Smuts Offensive	76
The Drive to Rufiji	90
The Remnant of an Army: 1917	95
The Long March: 1917-18	101

Chapter Four - Carrier Units

The Bishop of Zanzibar's Carrier Corps	112

The Uganda Carriers 124
The Kikuyu Mission Volunteers 135

Chapter Five - Carrier Welfare

Rations and Medicines 151
Two Officers in-charge of Carriers 163
Wages and Claims 173

Chapter Six - Effects of the War

Experience 186
Post-war Political Developments in Africa 196

Appendices

Appendix 1 - Carrier Corps Recruitment Statistics 211
   a) The East Africa Protectorate 211
   b) The Uganda Protectorate 213

Appendix 2 - Pay, Food and Equipment 216
   a) Examples of Monthly Pay for African Followers 216
   b) Improvements in Rations 217
   c) Clothing and Equipment 217

Appendix 3 - Some Medical Statistics 219
   a) The Uganda Transport Corps Carrier Section 219
   b) Deaths Between April and November 1917 220

Bibliography 221

Index 237

List of Plates

Plate 1: The War Memorial, Kenyatta Avenue, Nairobi. From left: Carrier, King's African Rifleman, Arab Rifleman .... Frontispiece

Plate 2: Lieutenant-Colonel O.F. Watkins, C.B.E., D.S.O., Director of Military Labour 20

Plate 3: A Nigerian Battery Carrier, with a 70lb. load, consisting of the wheel of a 2.95" mountain gun, its steel tyre being slung across his shoulder 50

Plate 4: A K.A.R. askari with a Vickers heavy machine gun 65

Plate 5: A K.A.R. column crossing a river, 1917 83

Plate 6: A Column of Carriers on the March in German East Africa 105

Plate 7: A Carrier Hospital, run by the Uganda African Native Medical Corps 131

Plate 8: A group of East Africa protectorate Carriers 142

Plate 9: "Grievously earned money." A sick Carrier, with a tropical ulcer 161

Plate 10: Kinyanjui wa Mukura and Nathaniel Mahingu 201

List of Tables and Maps

Table 1:	Africans Recruited by the British as Troops and Followers............	34
Table 2:	Logistics of Delivering One Ton of Stores a Day............	54
Table 3:	Number of Missing Men and the Unpaid Claims............	182
Map 1:	The East Africa Protectorate, 1914 to 1918: Areas of Recruitment and Military Operations............	40
Map 2:	German East Africa, showing the main Operations of 1914-1917, and the principal Lines of Communication....	79

Preface to the abridged Edition

After the publication of *the Carrier Corps* in the U.S.A., Geoffrey Hodges was keen to publish a second edition in Kenya to make it more accessible to people in East Africa, particularly secondary schools and undergraduate students. This would give a greater awareness and understanding of the value of the Carrier Corps in the East African Campaign of the First World War and the incredible hardships they suffered, many dying in service.

Geoffrey Hodges virtually rewrote the book, changing the title to *Kariakor* (a colloquial acronym of *Carrier Corps*), and abridging it, though this has been sparingly done so that most of the original material is still in this edition. He also added some new information that had come to light since the work was first published. Nairobi University Press agreed to publish the Second Edition. Regretfully, Geoffrey died soon after this arrangement was made. His widow, Gillian Hodges requested that the work of publishing the book continue and kindly asked me if I would take over the editing of the work which I have been pleased to do.

I have been able to make corrections and additions to the text mainly to make the references clearer and add to the understanding of the narrative. I have also added some further titles to the Bibliography, notably *Oscar from Africa* - the Biography of O.F. Watkins by his daughter, Elizabeth Watkins. Watkins was the administrator in charge of the Carrier Corps throughout the war and did a difficult job courageously and with distinction. Geoffrey had fortunately had access to the Watkins papers, and now that the papers have been published in the

Biography, they enhance the quality of *Kariakor's* Bibliography.

I am grateful to Gillian Hodges for her patience and encouragement to see the work published; also to Dr. Andrew Agnew of Aberystwith University, and a long time friend of the Hodges, for continued interest in furthering the publishing of this edition. Mr Omari Gichogo of Nairobi University Press has provided very friendly help and expertise in seeing the book through its various stages to completion.

I hope that this edition will be more readily available in East Africa and in other countries, and enjoy a wider reading public which it so richly deserves.

ROY GRIFFIN
November, 1999

Acknowledgements

By Geoffrey Hodges, for the Second Edition

Research on the "Carrier Corps" began in 1968; an unwieldy first draft was completed in 1973, but further work was impossible until 1978. A new draft was finished in 1979. My warm thanks go to Lesley Hopkins for her exquisitely drawn maps, and to Wendy Duggan for typing the first draft.

Researching and writing such a book, and getting it published, would have been totally impossible without the willing and generous help of many people, a fact one realises all the more when a book is about to be published. I am deeply indebted to Mrs. June Knowles for allowing me to use and quote from the personal papers of her father, Lieutenant-Colonel O.F. Watkins, C.B.E., D.S.O., who ran the Carrier Corps. I am very grateful indeed to Mrs. Elspeth Huxley for reading part of the first draft, and for her valuable suggestions. Miss Margaret Elington very kindly gave me copies of two relevant books, formerly belonging to her father, a pioneer settler in Kenya.

In Kenya, I am especially indebted, first, to Mr. David Sperling, Principal of Strathmore College, Nairobi, under whom I taught for six years, for much initial good advice, and latterly for help with various missing details; to Professor Alan Ogot, who as Head of the History Department at the University of Nairobi helped me with essential advice on sources and official procedures; to Dr. Brian McIntosh for his vital collection of Carrier documents in the Research Project Archives in the University Library; to Dr. Clive Irvine for so generously allowing me a free choice of his superb campaign photographs, which so much enhance the quality of this book; to Dr. Ralph

Scott, for personal reminiscences, friendly interest and the use of his library. I am very grateful also for the help and interest of Professor Godfrey Muriuki, Professor Gideon Were, Dr. Kenneth King, Dr. Ben Kipkorir, Dr. Terry Ryan, Dr. Gordon Jungeam and Dr. John Kieran. I am greatly indebted for their kindness and helpfulness to the following: Mr. N.W. Fedha and his staff at the Kenya National Archives, and the librarians and their staff at the McMillan Library, the University Library, the Welcome Library, the *East African Standard* and the Presbyterian Church of East Africa. I am also grateful for the help and advice of Archbishop Leonard Beecher, Mr. Edward Rodwell, Mr. John Nottingham and Mr. Keith Hardyman.

I owe an immeasurable debt of gratitude to all those friends who helped so willingly with field research, either as eyewitnesses - especially Mr. Jonathan Okwirri, Mr. Josiah Njonjo and Mr. James Beuttah - or as companions, guides, interpreters, translators of tapes and contributors of notes. Their names are recorded in the Bibliography and Sources, and without their kindly assistance this book would have been very much the poorer.

In Britain, I am deeply grateful to Dr. John Lonsdale for his guidance both with research, and with writing up the results; to Dr. A.T. Matson, Dr. Anthony Clayton, Dr. Richard Cashmore and Mr. S.H. Fazan for reading several chapters of the first draft, and for helping me freely with their wide knowledge and experience of Kenya and her history; to Mr. H.B. Thomas for some very valuable information and documentary sources, especially the *Military Labour Bureau Handbook* (after I had despaired of ever finding a copy); to Dr. Andrew Agnew, who read much of the first draft, and helped me to reduce its bulk; to

Dr. J. Forbes Munro for some valuable help with sources; to Mr. Charles Richards, for reading the second draft and making some important suggestions; to Professor George Shepperson for encouraging me to produce a new draft in 1978; to Professor Richard Gray and Dr. Andrew Roberts for welcoming me to a Conference on Africa and the First World War, at the School of Oriental and African Studies, and for their advice; to Professor Roland Oliver for vital help in finding a publisher; to Mr. Rex Collings; to Mr. Jeffery Ede (formerly Keeper of Manuscripts) and his staff at the Public Record Office, who helped me track down much essential material; to Mr. Donald Simpson, Librarian of the Royal Commonwealth Society, and his staff - his advice on sources and books has been immensely valuable; also to the librarians and staff at Rhodes House (Oxford), Edinburgh University Library, the Church Missionary Society and Central Africa House, both in London (the latter was then the headquarters of the former Universities' Mission to Central Africa, with whom I worked for five years in Zambia.)

Thanks are also due to the archivist at the Tanzania National Archives, and to the librarian at the University of Malawi. I would also like to thank two friends who long ago tutored me in elementary Luganda, and laid the foundations of an enduring interest in Africa: Mr. Ronald Snoxall and Mr. Ernest Sempebwa.

Last but not least, affection and gratitude are due to my wife ad daughters for constant quiet encouragement, and for their tolerance towards the unsociable behaviour which authorship seems bound to involve.

GEOFFREY HODGES, Aymestrey, Herefordshire,
May, 1986

By Mrs. Gillian Hodges, for the Second Edition

My daughter Nicola and I are pleased that a second edition of the "Carrier Corps" has been published. This brings to fruition what Geoffrey had always wanted. Before his death, he had initiated the publishing of the book with the Nairobi University Press to whom we are most grateful.

Our sincere thanks go to Roy Griffin, who had met Geoffrey, for agreeing to undertake the editing of this edition. Being resident in Nairobi and having access to several books, reports, and documents on East Africa, he has been valuable in the updating and editing of the manuscript and seeing it through to publication.

Dr. Andrew Agnew continued to be most helpful and brought the abridged manuscript to Nairobi and introduced Geoffrey and I to Roy.

We feel sure that this edition will reach a wider reading public, not only in East Africa but also in other countries.

GILLIAN HODGES
November 1999

Introduction

The Carrier Corps in History

The Carriers, who were the feet and hands of the army
(Rudyard Kipling)

The above words are part of the inscription on the War Memorial in Kenyatta Avenue, Nairobi, Kenya. They commemorate a great feat of courage and endurance by many thousands of Africans who fought as soldiers, or who toiled as followers, in the long drawn-out campaign to conquer German East Africa during the First World War (1914-1918). There, Africans showed courage and endurance equal to that of Europeans; and they often surpassed them.

Humanity's interest in stories of heroism began thousands of years before history became the academic discipline that it is today. Great sages, like Homer did not glorify war: they emphasised its tragedy, cruelty and wastefulness. They also inspired people with the heroic deeds of their ancestors. Indeed, history would be very boring if the epic side of it were omitted. To the African people therefore, the story of *the Carrier Corps*, the *King's African Rifles, the Schutztruppe,* and *the West African Frontier Force,* is about their forefathers' achievements with all their sorrow, suffering and glory.[1] These soldiers and followers not only showed great courage, but also a shrewd understanding of this fearful war and why the white men fought each other.

In the course of research for this book thirty years ago, we met old men who talked by the hour of what they saw, what they did and where they went. Their reminiscences, together with written accounts, bring to mind vivid pictures of reeking black mud and blinding red dust, of long columns of sweating, overloaded carriers, of sudden ambushes by the hidden enemy, of panicking porters dropping their loads and fleeing, of night assaults and the abandonment of half-cooked meals.

One can also visualise ammunition carriers or stretcher bearers trudging fatalistically up, to and back from the firing line, indifferent to danger, or perhaps even courting death. It was therefore, a tremendous privilege to meet some of these men and to record some of their memories. Very few survivors of the First World War are alive today in any country, and the African carriers and askaris are no exception. Nearly all of them are now dead. They have gone to join the great army that went so far from their homes, so many to their death, far, far, away from their loved ones.

Before the campaign, there were four German colonies in Africa: German East Africa (Tanganyika, now Tanzania), Togoland, the Cameroons and German South-West Africa, now Namibia. Togoland was overrun by the British and French by the end of August 1914 while German South-West Africa surrendered to the South Africans and Rhodesians in July 1915. The Cameroons, a much larger and more difficult country, held out until March 1916.[2] In this conflict, most of the fatal casualties recorded by the French and British, that is, over 4,000 soldiers, were caused by disease. This did not include mortality among carriers, which is estimated to be very high. Most of the dead succumbed to gastric disorders like dysentery and typhoid due to poor sanitation and camp indiscipline. This spectre reappeared on a more frightful scale during the conflict in

Introduction

German East Africa which was a much bigger campaign than the other three put together.

The story of the carrier corps is therefore one of great human interest and pathos. John Ainsworth, the veteran East Africa Protectorate administrator whose work was instrumental in making the recruitment of so much military labour possible, called the 1914-1918 a "Porters War", aptly summarising the whole situation.[3] No European who served in East Africa at that time would have disagreed with Ainsworth. There are many testimonials to the bravery, endurance and cheerfulness of the men of the *Carrier Corps*. Hence, the very name has a certain ring and buoyancy about it, lacking in the later ponderous military titles, conveying a fame which should be imperishable. As mentioned earlier, we are fortunate in that it has been possible to illustrate this from the reminiscences of the men who took part, and who were still alive when research on writing this book was being carried out in the late 1960s. They were willing to talk, not only of their experiences in the war, but also of going far afield to seek work before the war.[4] *They were indeed the feet and hands of the colonial armies.*

Notes

1. The *Schutztruppe* (Protection Troops) fought alongside the Germans while the Carrier Corps, the King's African Rifles and the West African Frontier Force were on the British ranks.
2. Charles Lucas, *The Empire at War* (London: on p. 1924), Vol. IV.
3. Public Record Office (London), Colonial Office 533/183/40516-7.
4. See "Oral Sources" in this book's Bibliography for a complete list of the survivors who talked to the author.

Chapter One

African Labour

Labour Before the War

I went away during the famine of the maize bags...I started building the railway from Mombasa up to Uganda
(Mwanyula Bikatana, Kaloleni, Giriama)

Since the beginning of agriculture 12,000 years ago, labour for most of the human race has meant a variety of personal activities centred on subsistence farming. River valley civilisations like those of the Nile, and of the great rivers of southern and eastern Asia involved great irrigation projects which meant the mass organisation of labour. These civilisations also produced vast works like the Egyptian pyramids or the Great wall of China. Chinese peasants dying in their thousands on the Great Wall were consoled with the thought that they were helping to keep out the nomad barbarians. The builders of the Pyramid of Cheops, of ancient British sanctuaries like Stonehenge, or of the Temple and Citadel of Great Zimbabwe may all have been driven by compelling religious motives. This sort of labour is not, of course, really voluntary; a subtle form of veiled compulsion known as "moral persuasion" comes into play. It often appears in the tangled story of colonial labour recruiting. Forced labour appeared early in ancient times, either in outright slavery, or in other forms of compulsion. Medieval Europe produced the feudal institution of serfdom, where land was held in return for compulsory labour.

African Labour

Until the beginning of the industrial revolution in the late eighteenth century, the majority of the human race practised subsistence agriculture. This was the way of life for most of the inhabitants of Africa when European colonisation began, and indeed it still is today. In the East Africa Protectorate, as in other parts of Africa, men did the heavy work such as clearing bush, breaking up new land, building huts and looking after livestock. This work was potentially dangerous if wild animals or human enemies attacked. Women cooked and did the housework, planted and reaped the crops, and carried the loads. As trade developed, they also marketed the produce. The growth of long-distance trade routes, contact with the coast and finally European colonisation, inevitably caused drastic interference with cherished customs. It has been much the same in Europe, as industrial and urban civilization has corroded country life.

The development of internal trade routes in central and eastern Africa presented peculiar problems which could only be overcome by the use of men and women to carry loads. In most land areas of the world, except the very mountainous, men could rely for long-distance transport on animals or on water, but in sub-equatorial Africa, river navigation was often unreliable, particularly in the eastern half of the continent. Trackless bush made the use of carts impossible and unreliable, while whenever it occurred, mostly in tropical Africa up to about 3,500 feet above sea level, tsetse fly ruled out horses, donkeys, mules, cattle or camels. This explains the lack of contact between the coast of East Africa and the interior until the first half of the nineteenth century.

The Muslim eivilization on the coast had begun about the 8th century AD. After 1804, the influence of the Sultan of Oman, Seyyid Said, spread along the coast and in the 1820s and 1830s, the Arab and Swahili caravans began to use the long established African trade routes to the interior. Thus began the great but short-lived tradition of the professional long-distance porters, recruited both from the coast Swahili, and from up-country people like the Nyamwezi. However, actual caravan portage did not take off until after 1840 when Seyyid Said moved his capital from Oman to Zanzibar. Then the demand for slaves rose rapidly as a result of the cloves plantations coinciding with the boom in the ivory trade. The next forty years were to become the golden age of European exploration, and although European interference with the slave trade meant the decline of Muslim trade with the interior, there were still opportunities for the professional porter.

After 1890, the European partition of East and Central Africa was virtually complete. This effectively cut off the Muslim traders from their partners up-country and destroyed the traditional pattern of commerce. The Sultan of Zanzibar accepted British protection, and was compensated for giving up his claims to the German share of the mainland. In the British sphere, he kept a ten-mile wide strip called *Seyidie* between the sea and the East Africa Protectorate, which gave its name to the whole coastal province. In 1890, the Muslim people of Zanzibar, Pemba, Mafia and the coast, who were still technically subjects of the Sultan, were forbidden by him to work outside his dominions. These developments destroyed the profession of the traditional caravan porter, but until the Uganda Railway reached Lake Victoria in 1901, porters were still needed to maintain this vital imperial line of communication between Mombasa and Uganda. They were increasingly recruited from up-country tribes who were steadily drawn into the economy of the coast.[1]

Load-carrying by men was contrary to tribal custom throughout most of Africa, but customs in any society change with times. The development of internal trade routes by people like the Kamba could hardly have been done without porter transport. However, local transport depended on women. For example, Kikuyu women carried heavy loads with their head straps; many still do. That is why in about 1903, people in Nyeri were amazed to see warriors behaving like women by carrying loads with head straps. The gender roles were so clearly defined that when at the outbreak of the war a District Officer in Northern Rhodesia, now Zambia, was explaining to a chief the need to recruit large numbers of porters to carry supplies to the German border, the chief agreed with an ironic remark : "When we go to war, our women carry for us. Now we shall do your women's work."[2]

While the carriage of loads on the head was usual throughout most of Africa, the head strap served a better method in mountainous country like Kikuyuland. It is commonly used in the Himalayas, where men have for many centuries carried loads of over 200 lbs in this way on long trade routes into Tibet and China over passes 20,000 feet above sea level. The elite of these high altitude porters are the famous Sherpas, without whom the feats of European mountaineers would never have been possible. In the same way, European exploration and military operations in Africa were totally dependent on African carriers, even if they were only pressed men. The upper limit for a head-load was probably 70 or 80 lbs, although 50 to 60 lbs was more usual. The art could be acquired through experience by those not used to it as the Carrier Corps. head-strap portage, on the other hand, could only be learned from practice in early childhood because the right muscles had to be developed in the neck. Consequently, Europeans had to use the less efficient method of shoulder straps, although one could ease the strain of a heavy rucksack using a head strap as well. Richard Meinertzhagen, who was working with the KAR, once bet with a certain official carrying nothing but his huge bulk, that a Swahili porter would beat him over eighteen miles with a sixty pound load; the porter won the wager by a mile.

By 1870, the Arab-Swahili economy on the coast was not only becoming transformed by the growing interest of western powers, but also by the increasingly strong participation of Indian merchants who introduced the rupee. It became the accepted currency on the East African coast. British railway engineers from India directed the construction of the Uganda Railway, but Indian labour built it in its earlier stages, while Indian artisans and clerks staffed it. Indian merchants accompanied its progress up-country, and established a permanent trading system.

The British colonisation of the new territories laid heavy demands on the African population, and also offered Africans opportunities which they quickly seized. The Swahili caravan route through Taveta was abandoned in favour of the old Kamba route through Tsavo and Kibwezi for the Uganda caravans, which then depended on two vital areas for food and carriers. The first of these was the southern Kikuyu District which later came to be known as Kiambu. Here, caravans were provisioned and porters provided for the march through the Rift Valley to the Luyia land in Northern Nyanza. In each of these, the British depended on an able local man who became the keystone of their administration: Kinyanjui in Kiambu, and Mumia among the Luyia. The tribal groups of modern Kenya are well known to be acephalous societies, amongst whom there were no dynasties of rulers, or traditional hierarchies of nobles. The British found Buganda with its king the Kabaka, a highly organised political system, much more comprehensible than the Luo, Luyia or Kikuyu with their complex systems of elders and age grades.

Before 1914, few Africans in the East Africa Protectorate worked away from home voluntarily. Growing numbers were forced to do so in order to find money to pay the white man's taxes, or to obey the newly imposed chiefs and headmen, whose duty was to fulfill government labour requirements. As the farming and trading community grew, so did demands for labour, but there is evidence that increasing numbers of young men were attracted by the novelty of this new way of life. One could get away from the restrictions of village life imposed by elders and custom to be free, see the world and meet new people. If you went out, on your own, you could make your own terms with a farmer or other employer of your own choice and earn money to buy new and exciting things from traders. If you did not like your employer, you could leave him and find someone more suitable who paid you more or treated you better.

One of our informants, Elijah Kaara, came from Mihuti in South Tetu, Nyeri District. He said that a number of the *njaange rika* (roam age grade) of 1901 went to Nairobi as the railway approached that site and returned home with a kind of cloth fashionable at dances. He also wanted such cloth. He decided to earn some money and therefore went to Nairobi where he worked as a kitchen boy. Later, he became a clerk at the Nairobi Carrier Depot, then a storeman in German East Africa. After the war, he worked in South Tetu for the Kikuyu Central Association. Josphat Njoroge, another of our informants, worked on a farm in Kiambu but was only paid Rs.3 (3 rupees), whereas others were getting Rs.4. So he decided to work for another European as a cook for six months before going home to be circumcised. In 1917, he served with the Kikuyu Mission Volunteers. In these two examples, the men concerned may have left home for economic reasons but were to some extent, able to please themselves as to what they did, or where they went.

Towards the end of the nineteenth century, many left home because of famine. For example, Mwanyula Bikatana, whose home was at Kaloleni in Giriama left home in 1899 because of the "famine of the maize bags", and worked on the Uganda Railway until it reached Kisumu.[3] He then lived in German East Africa but after the outbreak of war, he was conscripted as an ammunition carrier in the German forces. He was taken prisoner by the British in Portuguese East Africa, and finally returned home.

It is unlikely that many worked willingly as carriers, except perhaps with hunting safaris, which became popular with wealthy European and American visitors. The prospect of feasting on meat attracted many young men, except perhaps Kikuyus who were said to dislike game flesh. It was a healthy life; the comparatively small numbers of men were constantly on the move, and so they did not foul the ground or overburden water supplies. Conditions were much less healthy on military expeditions though, as exemplified by the Nandi campaign of 1894 and the Uganda caravan disaster of 1899. Thousands of carriers from Nyanza had to go to Turkana, which was not pleasant and even after the outbreak of war, 4,000 of them were sent there. Then there were the constant safaris from Nyeri and Meru with food suppliers to Archer's Post to sustain military operations in the Northern Frontier District and also the porters for government work within districts. By 1914, the uncongenial work of carrying loads must have been widely familiar, however disliked.

Labour conditions were frequently bad, particularly in the area of housing, rations, medical care, and discipline. This came out forcefully in the evidence of many witnesses before the Native Labour Commission of 1912 to 1913 which was composed of African chiefs and headmen, missionaries, doctors, government officers and farmers. Examples of work places where conditions were specially disliked were the Magadi railway and soda works, ballast-breaking on the railway, the Mombasa waterworks, and sisal plantations in general where the spines caused septic wounds.

Grim evidence about the medical unfitness of the African population was given by Dr. H.R.A. Philp, a Church of Scotland medical missionary at Tumutumu, in Nyeri District. He reported that 40% of the people living north of Tana River were unfit for labour. The government's failure to drain the swamps along the Fort Hall-Nairobi road caused migrant workers to die of malaria.[4] This was borne out by a complaint in the *East African Standard* by a settler, Major James Elkington, about dead bodies lying by the roadside. Later, Philp's evidence was corroborated by John Ainsworth, the then Provincial Commissioner for Nyanza and a leading expert on labour in the East Africa Protectorate, and also by Norman Leys a government medical officer. Officials like Ainsworth and O.F. Watkins, and missionaries like Philp and A.R. Barlow, knew much more about African living conditions and diet than most settlers did.

It was, however, an enlightened settler who quoted an impassioned outburst by Ainsworth against the callous disregard for labourers and their welfare shown by some employers. A drafty hut, a thin blanket, and a minimum ration of maize or *matama* meal were clearly not good enough, especially for men used to a warmer climate. At times, there was no one to cook for the workers or to look after them. Ainsworth thought that the only answer was to ensure that "those ignorant white employers" got no labourers at all until they learned to treat them decently.[5] He recommended that a Native Affairs Department be established to instil high professional standards in African welfare and labour management, especially in rations and a medical care.[6] Ainsworth's advice was however not followed by the government. As a result, there was no criteria for proper management of military labour by 1914. It is therefore not difficult to imagine the fatal results when thousands of carriers were recruited on the outbreak of war.

The East Africa Protectorate was much more closely administered than any other British territory and thus better able to produce labour, almost resembling German East Africa. Hence, there were far more government records of carrier recruiting than existed in any other country in East Africa. This fact gave a rather lop-sided view of the whole subject.

The picture on the eve of the great war is therefore, a complicated one. Most labour was not voluntary, but undoubtedly, some men made a virtue of necessity and out of their own volition, went to find work, especially those from the Kikuyu and Nyanza Districts. Working conditions were generally bad, and no proper administrative standards existed for the care of labourers. Many officials, settlers and missionaries were acutely aware of this when the Labour Commission reported it in 1913. It was however too late to do anything about Ainsworth's recommendations and to make some difference before the beginning of the war in 1914.

The wartime sufferings of the Carrier Corps had two roots. First, from the British colonial governments which had no departments to lay down and enforce proper conditions for African labour in peacetime. Secondly, from the military department where there was neither adequate military planning for a war with Germany in East Africa, nor adequate planning for the transport which would be required.

The Carrier Corps

"The whistling of the bullets could be heard in the air; Siuu! Siuu! " (Nguku Mulwa, syce)

"War is a stupid and brutal business which no man would wish to see repeated." This was the verdict of Field Marshal Erwin Rommel, admired as much by British soldiers in the Second World war as was General von Lettow-Vorbeck in the First. It is, however, true that war can bring out the finest qualities in people, as well as the most bestial.

The *Carrier Corps* was a military unit or formation like any battalion, regiment, or corps, except that it was vastly larger. Very few of its men wore anything like a normal military uniform. They had no boots, or indeed little but a blanket, like the bronze carrier on the War Memorial in Kenyatta Avenue, Nairobi. Although they were not fighting-men, they were entitled to the protection of their officers, and eventually to the same rations and welfare arrangements as the soldiers. The unit existed for the duration of the 1914-1918 Great War in East Africa, but unlike the King's African Rifles (KAR), it was disbanded at the end of that war.[7]

The first carrier depot was in Nairobi, on the site of the present *Kariakor* Market, which together with the War Memorial, serve to remind us of the tragedy of war. There is a corresponding *Kariakor* in Mombasa, and a suburb in Dar es Salaam called *Kariakoo* (the two are colloquial acronyms of "Carrier Corps") The young men of an entire generation, if they were medically fit, passed through the Nairobi Carrier Depot from the Central, Ukambani and Nyanza Provinces of the East Africa Protectorate; and from Uganda via smaller bases like Kisumu. The Nairobi Carrier Depot was the centre of pay and registration system where the Carrier Corps was administered. It was also the main carrier hospital where research vital to the health of men, hundreds of miles away in the heart of German territory was carried out. It should be emphasized that this complex organisation was not responsible for the large southern carrier forces, nor for military railway labour, for whom no statistics seem to have survived. The Mombasa depot received labour for Kilindini Docks, and acted as a clearing house for labour passing through on their way to or from the German ports. After the capture of Dar es Salaam in 1916, a major carrier Depot was established there. Voi was a key depot in 1915 when preparations were in progress for the 1916 offensive, after which it became less important.

During the twenty-five years between the funding of British administration by the Imperial British East Africa Company and the outbreak of the Great War, the British had plenty of experience in portage, both with the Uganda caravans of the 1890s, and in various local campaigns. The main lesson was that appalling mortality could result from intestinal diseases caused either by an unfamiliar diet, or by unsanitary conditions, or both. Despite this, there was in 1914 no military transport service, or even a plan for one, although the conquest of the German colonies in the event of war was an accepted aim of British imperial policy.

The Carrier Corps was therefore started with no administrative foundations and these had to be improvised by a team of administrative officers in charge. They were to have an uphill struggle against the ignorance and obstructiveness of the Indian Army staff, and of the settler-dominated Central Committee of Supply. With the aid of medical officers many of whom came from South Africa, their professional expertise in African dietary requirements was gradually established. The mining companies in South Africa and Rhodesia were many years ahead of East Africa in this vital area of labour management.

While the major land campaigns of the 1914 to 1918 War were fought either on European soil, or in the Ottoman Empire in the Middle East, the conquest of German East Africa was the only possible exception. Here alone, the numbers of men involved went over the one million mark. The British imperial forces numbered about 120,000 soldiers: African, Indian, South African, Rhodesian, British and West Indian, in about that order. Over half of this number were Africans.[8]

If we assume that each soldier was supported by ten followers of all kinds, then the military labour forces needed to sustain all these troops in a difficult tropical country must have numbered over a million. The Belgians advanced from their recently acquired colony (which was then called the Belgian Congo but is now known as The Democratic Republic of Congo) with about 10,000 African troops and a large number of carriers, nearly 130,000 provided by the British authorities in Uganda. About 120,000 of these men were described as unorganised "job porters" for the Belgian advance; 8,429 were a force raised for the 1916 advance, and were known as the Belgian Congo Carrier Corps although they were Ugandan men. Uganda also sent 3,576 men to Nairobi in 1914 for the East Africa Carrier Corps (as the first military labour force in the Northern British Protectorates was called). Uganda produced some 50,000 more followers during the course of the war, and 10,000 troops.

This record of Uganda's contribution reveals several important issues which need to be understood about military labourers or followers. First, a large proportion of those raised for the East African campaign served temporarily or seasonally, and were controlled throughout by government officers in the various territories concerned. Hence, it is questionable how far they can really be called "military". Nyasaland and Northern Rhodesia (as Malawi and Zambia were then called) produced about 250,000 followers, of whom perhaps 80% worked seasonally or on a sort of shift system on the very long line of communication running through these countries to the German border. A number of them either worked from home or never moved very far away.

Secondly, this also applies to some of those followers who were under military discipline, who only worked locally, and for a few months or less at a time. Others, on the other hand, served for two years or more in totally strange countries many hundreds of miles from home, and with no certain prospects of ever returning. Under such circumstances, sick men lost the will to live. This group included the front-line porters, machine-gun and ammunition carriers, and stretcher bearers whose work added deadly danger to heavy labour. The statistics show that of the British territories, the majority of these men came from the East Africa Protectorate (as Kenya was then called).

Thirdly, the word "follower" is best when discussing non-combatants in general, because carrying loads was only one of the many things they had to do. Men might be carriers one day, and the next day would have to dig drains, build bridges, make roads, put up huts, or repair a railway line. Apart from the special duties personnel, there were also interpreters, armed scouts, carriers, police, telegraph workers, intelligence agents, dock workers, technicians, grooms and animal drivers. Others were ward orderlies, dressers, cooks and personal servants.

The East Africa Carrier Corps was the title of the first such unit. It was formed in the East Africa Protectorate and its first depot was in Nairobi. Any study of military labour in East Africa is therefore bound to have a bias towards the northern territories, particularly the East Africa Protectorate whose administration was more highly organised than any other for the recruitment of labour. At the end of 1914, the East Africa Protectorate and Uganda had separate transport corps, each with its own carrier section.

In 1916, before Field-Marshal J.C. Smuts' great offensive, all followers of every kind were placed under the control of a new organisation called the Military Labour Bureau. This dull and inappropriate title conceals the fact that the vast majority of its huge membership were on active service. The Military Labour Bureau was responsible for all followers on the northern front, but not for men working under the Belgians, on the railways which with the exception of the Uganda Railway, were under military control or on Nyasaland and Northern Rhodesia fronts.

The British had failed to destroy the German forces by 1916. The 1917 offensive gave them the south-eastern corner of the German colony, but the Germans escaped into Portuguese territory. The operations involved raising nearly 120,000 carriers, mostly in the East Africa Protectorate, Uganda and the occupied areas of German East Africa. The East African Force, advancing from the north, took over the southern columns with their troops and followers in March 1918. *The Military Labour Bureau* was belatedly called The Military Labour Corps although the most active phase of its existence was over. The number of followers fell far below what they had been in the middle of 1917 when very few members of the formerly large southern forces were still in service. *The Military Labour Corps* presided over the final and most bureaucratic phase of Carrier Corps history.

A grim struggle was waged by the officers of the carrier corps (under whichever of its titles) with the officers of the fighting units who were forever interfering with the discipline, control and management of the carriers. The standard was set by the group of administrative officers seconded by the East Africa Protectorate and Uganda Governments who started the original Carrier Corps in 1914. Though they were soon granted military rank, they considered themselves responsible to their governments for the welfare of their men.

This account of the Carrier Corps cannot possibly describe every action or battle in which the unit took part as a normal regimental history would, for sheer lack of evidence. The official history of the KAR is literally a blow-by-blow account of its subject. As we have seen, the Carrier Corps as a military unit was mainly based in the northern territories of East Africa. But its story is, however, much more than simply a chapter of military history; for apart from the military history and its administrative divisions, the strategic situation before the war caused by the rivalries of the great European powers must be considered.

The development of a British government in the East Africa Protectorate forms part of the plot. It was geared more and more towards producing labour for the government; for Uganda Railway and Kilindini Docks, and for private employers of every conceivable kind. Labour recruitment caused major problems in the management and in the humane treatment of labour. These involved the feeding and medical care of African workers from different tribes with widely varying dietary habits, and often working in unfamiliar climatic conditions. Problems of labour recruitment and management, difficult enough before the war, increased enormously with the ever-growing demands for military labour.

Nevertheless, the expansion of the war into German territory, and the insatiable military demands for more and more labour in 1916 and 1917, resulted in a ghastly loss of life despite all improvements in administration, rations and medical care. Mortality amongst front-line carriers was over 20%, including the missing as well as the dead. On lines of communication where many thousands laboured in the peak years, it decreased as organisation improved. The average death rate was probably

Lieutenant-Colonel O.F. Watkins, C.B.E., D.S.O., Director of Military Labour

Courtesy of Mrs. E.J.F. Knowles

about 10% of all military followers; but as there were over 1,000,000 carriers of all kinds and on all fronts, the total mortality was well over 100,000. This does not include the very large numbers who died of their sufferings after repatriation, nor any recruited by the Belgians or Portuguese.

This terrible loss of life amongst the young men of a whole generation must have had very far-reaching and traumatic effects on the social, economic and emotional life of the African countries involved. This was especially so in German East Africa, which was the main battlefield, where men were forced to work first for the Germans and then for the British. Yet, historians of the East African campaign have tended to concentrate very much on the military details. They have said very little indeed about the military followers, without whom the campaigns could never have been fought at all. As a military unit, the Carrier Corps was twice as big as all the others put together.

Ironically, the campaign in East Africa has been seen by Europeans as something of a light relief when compared with the grim mass slaughter on the Western Front. It gave scope for colourful adventurers like Spicer-Simson who won naval command of Lake Tanganyika with two motor boats dragged by steam engines across hundreds of miles of bush and mountain, a feat which would have been impossible without African labour.

Other remarkable individuals were Selous and Pretorius, (both famous big game hunters); Drought with his Skin Corps, Meinertzhagen and his intelligence scouts, and Wavell who led the Arab Rifles. Paul von Lettow-Vorbeck, the German Commander, was unbeaten when he surrendered a day after the armistice, and has a good claim to be the most successful

German general of the war. He was devotedly served by his elite corps of askaris and porters.

As the commander of the Carrier Corps throughout the war, Oscar Ferris Watkins too has a good claim to a place among the outstanding men of the campaign although his name never features in these orthodox accounts. Another is John Ainsworth, the veteran East Africa Protectorate administrator whose work, particularly in the Nyanza Province, was instrumental in making the recruitment of so much military labour possible, and to whom Watkins owes enormous debt for advice and support. Ainsworth was the only man to direct the mass levy in 1917. Undoubtedly, all these remarkable Europeans owed their successes partly to African scouts, hunters, carriers and soldiers.

Notes

[1] Matson, *Nandi Resistance*, 192.
[2] Public Record Office, Cabinet Office Papers 45/14,8.
[3] Interview at Kaloleni, Giriama, 24 Jan. 1970.
[4] Native Labour Commission, 1912-1913, 203-207; letter from James Elkington to *The Leader*, 21 Aug. 1911.
[5] Kenya National Archives, Provincial Commissioner, Nyanza/2/3, Ainsworth to Chief Secretary, 9 Oct 1912.
[6] Kenya National Archives - Provincial Commissioner, Nyanza/2/3. Ainsworth's "Memorandum on Native Affairs" 11 April, 1914; see also European witnesses to Native Labour Commission, 1912-1913.
[7] H. Moyse-Bartlett, *The King's African Rifles* (Aldershot: Gale and Polden, 1956).
[8] See "Report by Lieutenant-Colonel O.F. Watkins, C.B.E., D.S.O., Director of Military Labour" (typescript, Nairobi, 1919) - short title.

Chapter Two

The War Strategy

Gutiri undu utari kihumo -There is nothing without a root cause
(Kikuyu Proverb)

British Imperial Strategy

There is a traditional joke that the British are never prepared for war. Unfortunately, this has usually been true. In fact, none of the European colonial governments were really ready for war because an international agreement made thirty years earlier had declared that in the event of war in Europe, colonies in tropical Africa would remain neutral. This was the Berlin Act of 1885, which arose out of the conference convened by Bismarck, the Imperial German Chancellor.[1] In 1914, the last thing that European colonial governors in tropical Africa wanted was war. They feared it would upset all their development plans and perhaps provoke risings among their African populations.

By 1897, the British were becoming uneasily aware that the new Germany was hostile to them. In that year, Kaiser William II publicly congratulated President Kruger of the Transvaal for suppressing the uprising sponsored by Cecil Rhodes. Later, the new German Navy was directed against Britain. Accordingly, the War Office ordered plans to be drawn up for the invasion of German colonies should war break out. It came out with *"The Scheme for Operations against German East Africa 1897"* which was produced by the Director of Intelligence, Indian

Army. By then, the Indian Government was responsible for the defence of British territories in Eastern Africa. It retained this role until 1916 with profound consequences for the campaign in German East Africa.

The plan for the offensive

The main offensive would be based in Voi where the Uganda Railway had now reached. From there, Moshi and the German side of Kilimanjaro could be occupied. Then the German ports of Tanga, Bagamoyo and Dar es Salaam would be simultaneously seized. East African, Sudanese and Indian troops would be used, with mules, camels and Nyasaland carriers for transport. The seaborne attacks, the naval blockade, diversionary attacks from Uganda and, with luck, risings against the Germans would make the conquest of German East Africa reasonably easy.

There were five main flaws in this plan. One was the failure to foresee that carriers were the only reliable form of transport in a country where tsetse fly was very common. Secondly, the assumption that the Uganda Railway would be protected from German raids by the waterless country to the south proved to be false. Thirdly, the Germans in fact had no trouble from uprisings after the devastating suppression of the Maji Maji rebellion in 1906.[2] Fourthly, Indian troops proved much less suitable than Africans for East Africa operations. Finally, there was the fatal tendency to underrate the Germans and their determination to defend their colony.

In 1897, the Sudanese troops in Uganda mutinied; an event which threatened the whole British position in East Africa and challenged much of the thinking behind the plan for the conquest of German East Africa. There followed a severe lesson in African military transport problems which was ignored by the War Office. The first reinforcement for the hard-pressed Uganda Rifles were 400 Sikhs and Punjabis, followed by the 27th Bombay Light Infantry with twelve European officers and 737 Baluchi sepoys. This regiment reached railhead at Ndi, 120 miles from Mombasa, near the area where the famous man-eating lions had delayed railway construction. The troops were taken to Machakos by Nyika and Taita porters, and to Fort Smith by the Kamba. In 1895, there was a massacre by the Maasai at Kedong. Consequently, it was still difficult to get Kikuyu porters for the next stage to Naivasha and Ravine. The resources of the road up-country were thus severely overstretched considering that a famine and a smallpox epidemic were raging at the time. The demand for porters was all the greater because the sepoys' food had to be imported and brought up to railhead from Mombasa.

In 1899, the 27th BLI returned from Uganda to railhead, which was now at Kiu, on the eastern edge of the Kapiti Plains. They were accompanied by an enormous caravan of Ganda and Soga porters, 3,700 strong. Nyanza men could not be used, as being scantily clothed, they tended to die of cold on the 9,000 foot crossing of the Maw Escarpment. As they reached Athi River, hundreds were dying of dysentery and exhaustion under the horrified eyes of John Ainsworth and two other famous administrators, Charles Hobley and Francis Hall. Ainsworth did not blame Grant, the Uganda officer in charge. He thought the cause was the change from their usual diet of plantations to rice, which they did not know how to cook. They may have eaten it undercooked, which was dangerous, especially if it was allowed to ferment.

This dreadful tragedy showed clearly what could happen if military operations demanded exceptional numbers of carriers without proper administrative support. There was an epidemic on the Nandi expedition in 1895 which together with this dreadful tragedy, impressed itself on the minds of government officers like Ainsworth and Hobley; but it seems to have made no impact in Whitehall. A further lesson was that Indian troops could not be fed off the land, which greatly reduced their mobility. An Indian soldier cost more than an African and needed four times as much baggage, not counting transport necessary for rations. After the Sudanese Mutiny and its ghastly aftermath, it was obvious to officers with East African experience that Indian troops, being so expensive in transport, were less suitable than Africans for operations in Africa. In any case, Indian Government disliked having to send their troops.

In 1900, the last Asante campaign in the Gold Coast had shown the true value of African troops, and existing units were amalgamated into the West African Frontier Force. Troops in Nyasaland, Uganda, the East Africa Protectorate and Somaliland were similarly organised as the King's African Rifles in 1901. There were six battalions: the 1st and 2nd (Nyasaland), the 3rd (East Africa Protectorate), the 4th and 5th (Uganda) and the 6th (Somaliland). These units were all led by picked British officers, well trained and well armed with modern enfield magazine rifles of .303 calibre, replacing the obsolete Martini Henry single-shot .450 weapon.

There were serious limitations to the effectiveness of the European military officers when it came to war. They were under the Colonial Office whose powers were purely advisory, and not under the War Office. They were used as military police, for suppressing tribal disorder, rather than as troops. They tended to be scattered about in small detachments, especially in the East Africa Protectorate, where there was permanent unrest in the vast northern regions of Turkana, the Northern Frontier District and Jubaland. A KAR company consisted of two or three European officers, with 75 to 130 riflemen. Although there were no European non-commissioned officers (NCOs), this deficiency was made up by Sudanese veterans, known also as Nubians whose experience went back to the days of the Mahdi, the Khalifa, Emin Pasha and Kitchener. The KAR were seldom trained or worked together as battalions, and they had no permanent establishment of front-line carriers.

The German Schutztruppe (Protection Troops) were organised in companies of 160 rifles, with about twenty European officers and NCOs and 250 permanent carriers. Such companies were self-contained fighting units or flying columns, forged in the ruthless bush fighting of the Maji Maji Rebellion. A serious disadvantage compared with the KAR was that as late as 1912, they were still armed mainly with .450 single-shot rifles of 1871 pattern, which also used black powder, producing smoke which gave away the rifleman's position. The ammunition was also heavier than the .303 or 9mm type, and required more transport.

During his service with the KAR (1902-1906), Richard Meinertzhagen twice went on intelligence missions. He stayed with the German commanding officer at Moshi, and had a close look at the Schutztruppe. He thought they were as good as the KAR, but they were held together by iron discipline rather than by genuine friendship which bound officers and men in the KAR. "War alone can prove which is the most effective," Meinertzhagen concluded.[3]

After 1900, the British Government was becoming increasingly concerned about possible German aggression. Consequently, a Committee of Imperial Defence was set up in 1904. There was now less complacency about the security of the Uganda Railway, and as early as 1901, the two East African governments were being warned of those points which might be in danger of attack. By the time of Meinertzhagen's visit to Moshi, the main precept of the 1897 scheme was well understood - that the main offensive against German East Africa would be from Voi to Moshi.

Meinertzhagen's comments probably reflected the opinion of the Committee of Imperial Defence about the 1897 plan which was as follows: the Taveta salient would be untenable, having eighty miles of waterless country behind it. A railway would therefore have to be built from Voi. The general view of senior officers, including Lord Kitchener, who became Secretary for War in 1914, and who strongly objected to committing resources to a side-show like East Africa, was that the invasion of German East Africa would be a task out of all proportion to its importance [because] the real decision in any Anglo-German war would be arrived at in Europe, and not in Africa.

The Germans for their part agreed entirely. The General Staff had been told confidentially in 1906 that the colonies would not be defended if war came. The German commander in East Africa in 1914, Colonel Paul von Lettow-Vorbeck, understood this. He wrote after the war: "I knew that the fate of the colonies ... would be decided only on the battlefields of Europe",[4] Like his colleagues in the other African colonies, he nevertheless decided that it was his duty to help the Fatherland by waging war. However, they would be on their own. This was why wireless stations were built linking Berlin and the colonies. If war broke out, the Royal Navy would dominate all the sea routes, enforcing a blockade which would be difficult to break. Events would later prove the tenacity of their defence: South-West Africa held out for eleven months, and the Cameroons for eighteen; although Togoland fell within a month.

The neutrality doctrine of the Berlin Act was accepted by all colonial governments in tropical Africa and by most European settlers. This explains the dislike of the Colonial Office for any military activities from strategic planning to intelligence work, which implied that the Berlin doctrine might break down. In 1905, the Deputy Commissioner in Uganda commented that fears of possible German aggression had been derided, but that allusions to such a contingency, though very discreetly made, were sufficiently distinct. According to Charles Hobley, who was Provincial Commissioner at Mombasa before and during the war, some Germans behaved as if the East Africa Protectorate was virtually theirs by right. This hardly encouraged wishful thinking about German intentions.

The Boer War had shown the need for drastic army reforms which were passed in 1907.[5] The creation of the Imperial General Staff was long overdue, but the British army still depended on volunteers, not conscripts. The KAR remained under the Colonial Office, and in 1910, the 2nd, 5th and 6th battalions were disbanded. The British government wanted to reduce its grant, and the settlers in Nyasaland and the East Africa Protectorate were reluctant to shoulder the defence costs.

Oddly enough, the governors concerned were both former army officers. In Nyasaland, Sir William Manning had been Inspector-General for the KAR. In the East Africa Protectorate, Sir Percy

Girouard had been with Kitchener in the Sudan. His successor, Sir Henry Belfield, was not a solder, but in 1913, he took the adverse report on the KAR made by Colonel Thesiger, the Inspector-General, very seriously indeed. Lieut-Colonel Graham, commanding 3rd KAR, emphatically agreed, saying that it would be up to the local forces to stop the East Africa Protectorate from being overrun. A comment from a Whitehall official showed an amazing remoteness from strategic realities: "Rubbish - who is going to overrun E.A.?"[6]

In 1911, the War Office was advised to set up an intelligence government in the interests of a pacific policy. Thesiger's successor, Colonel A.R. Hoskins, who was Commander-in-Chief in East Africa for the first half of 1917, proposed a new Nyasaland battalion and a reserve of 500 men in two flying columns to guard the Uganda railway. This was approved but not implemented before war actually came.

In pre-war years, intelligence was gleaned by consular officials, by officers on shooting trips, and more seriously by District Officers in charge of border areas like Taveta, a Sub-District of Voi. The officer who was there in 1914, S. H. La Fontaine, skilfully withdrew most of his men after inflicting some losses upon the enemy. He then became an intelligence officer with the East African Force. Intelligence work depended upon Africans every bit as much as did transport. It was they who were to run appalling risks as agents in enemy territory. An intelligence service was as vital as a transport corps, but nothing was done to create one. However, the deficiency was rapidly made good when war actually broke out.

In his post-war report on military labour, Lieut-Colonel Watkins noted that in 1914, there were hardly any military instructions on that speciality of African warfare - carrier transport on a large scale, and that, local defensive arrangements had apparently never envisaged the possibility of a long line of communications by carriers; or of operations on any scale larger than a few companies.[7] Yet, a *Carrier Corps* was to be formed with remarkable speed as we shall see in the next section.

On their part, the KAR were, through no fault of theirs, not fit for war in 1914 but within a few months, they proved themselves to be the most effective troops under British command. The fact remains that Africans, who were vital as soldiers, carriers and intelligence agents, responded heroically to the challenge in 1914. Without their participation, the European war effort would have been in vain.

In November 1914, the British attempted to take Tanga, the northernmost port of German East Africa. The plan was drawn up by a committee of officials of the Colonial Office, India Office and Admiralty. Incredibly, the plan was not submitted to the General Staff. The Indian Government accordingly provided two expeditionary forces for East Africa known as *B* and *C*. While *A* force went to Mesopotamia, *C* force went up-country to guard the Uganda Railway. *B* force, which made the seaborne assault on Tanga, consisted of about 8,000 troops, mostly Indians but it also included one British battalion, the 2nd Loyal North Lancashire Regiment.

Major-General Aitken, commanding *B* force, had the chance of leaving his less reliable Indian units behind at Mombasa. He could have taken a picked force to Tanga including the Loyals, his best Indian units, marines from the warships and a contingent of 3rd KAR, which was offered by its commanding officer, Lieut-Colonel Graham. Aitken's refusal of this offer is impossible to excuse. The Germans at Tanga were given twenty-four hours warning of the attack which was totally unnecessary since Britain and Germany had been at war for three months. Consequently, von Lettow soon brought his troops from Moshi by train to Tanga, where he was finally able to assemble about 350 Europeans and 1,300 askaris.

The landing was made some distance away instead of in the harbour itself. The captain of HMS Fox, a light cruiser, refused to land there because of a false alarm about mines. When the fighting started, the untrained Indian troops panicked but even then, Aitken could have defeated von Lettow with a little determination as the German was inferior in numbers and had no artillery. In the end, Aitken withdrew with 360 men having been killed. He however got eight machine guns, 455 rifles and 600,000 rounds of ammunition, enough to equip two companies of askaris. Lettow lost 69 through deaths, but his shattering victory gave him the authority which he needed to wage war. He would later write,

> "[Could we] prevent considerable numbers of the enemy from intervening in Europe... or inflict on our enemies any loss of personnel or war material worth mentioning? I answered this question in the affirmative."[8]

In Tanga, there was a decisive battle. The damage to British morale and to Britain's reputation took years to repair. Von Lettow never really lost the initiative which he had gained at Tanga. With Tanga in British hands, it would have been much harder for the Germans to invade Gazi or Vanga District, or to attack the Uganda Railway. There were 2,000 Zanzibari carriers for the expected advance inland. Their appalling sufferings as they drifted about in open lighters for two days in the full heat of the sun without food and with very little water were later described by a British medical officer, whose ship took them in tow.

In 1914, when the fatal crisis occurred in Europe, the chiefs of staff of Austria, Germany and Russia forced their Emperors to agree that only the military option, expressed in their various war plans, could save the state. By the end of the year, all these plans had failed and so had the French plan. The British plan to conquer German East Africa also failed. Von Lettow similarly imposed his will on von Schnee, but his plan was simply to concentrate, and to take brilliant advantage of the many and grave errors committed by the British.

British imperial strategy was bound to be in a muddle when so many different agencies were expected to work in harmony. The Colonial Office supervised the civilian governments, the KAR and defence, advised by the War Office. The Indian Government, represented in London by the India Office, had to provide troops for East Africa. Ultimately, the defence of the largest sea-based empire in history depended on the Admiralty and the Royal Navy.

Recruiting in East Africa Protectorate

When they were caught by force, we were left weeping, mourning . (A woman viewpoint: Leah Nyamuiru Karuga, Kiambu District)

We know more about recruiting in the East Africa Protectorate, as Kenya was then called, than in other territories, none of which had a provincial administration as highly geared for raising labour. There are reports and statistics in the Kenya National Archives from the Protectorate's four provinces where porters were recruited. Nyanza produced 92,037, over twice the total of the other three. Its districts were North, Central (or Kisumu) and South Nyanza, Nandi and Lumbwa. Kenia comprised Murang'a, Nyeri, Embu and Meru. Ukamba included Machakos, Kitui, Kiambu and Nairobi. Seyidie consisted of Malindi, Nyika, Mombasa, Vanga and Taita. In Kenya we entirely rely on information from provincial records because the Secretariat Archives were destroyed by fire in 1938.

The British raised nearly 58,000 troops and about a million followers from fifteen African countries for their forces in East Africa. This statistical sample shows the number produced by the four leading countries from 1914 to 1918:

Table 1: Africans Recruited by the British as Troops and Followers

	Troops	Followers			
		Special Porter	Carriers	Casual Labourer	Total Followers
German East Africa	2,000	44,031	191,719	125,817	321,567
Nyasaland	15,000	unknown	195,652	1,262	196,914
E.A. Protectorate	10,500	16,611	145,967	10,961	173,539
Uganda	10,000	989	182,014	1,243	184,246

Of the followers, Kenia Province about 70% from German East Africa and a large minority from Nyasaland served seasonally or for short periods. The same applies to some 120,000 "job porters" raised in Uganda for the Belgians. It is not known how many of the Nyasaland carriers were special porters for carrying machine-guns, signal equipment, parts of mountain guns, stretchers, mortars and ammunition. They could have been about 5,000. Military Labour Bureau records provide the numbers for casuals, other numbers for German East Africa and the East Africa Protectorate. For Uganda, only 10,947 carriers and special porters were recruited for the mass levy in 1917. Apart from casuals, East Africa Protectorate followers served for longer terms, many over two years, and went further from home than any others. This explains their death rate of 14.6%, higher than the other three, as also does the fact that the East Africa Protectorate produced more special porters than all the rest put together. The Germans, however, conscripted thousands of their subjects who then had to work for the British.

During the campaign, there were four phases of recruiting. First, there was the pre-war system whereby labour was partly compulsory, partly voluntary. Then in 1915, the Native Followers Recruitment Ordinance brought general compulsion whereby Europeans and Asians were also conscripted. Next came the mass levy from March to August 1917, when it was abandoned partly because of the shortage of fit men. Military demands also dropped and the pre-war system returned.

The war gave fresh opportunities to the settlers of exerting pressure on government through the Committees of Supply and the War Council. They wanted more representation, more land and Crown Colony status for the Protectorate. Owing to the growth of African literacy, these demands, loudly voiced through the press, caused alarm for some years before the war not only among the Kikuyu but among the Luo in Nyanza, as Senior Chief Jonathan Okwirri told the author in 1970.

The main concern of all employers during the war was the labour supply. Farmers, sisal and coconut planters, the business community, the provincial administration, the Public Works Department, the Uganda Railway, the Kilindini Docks, the Magadi Soda Company, had all been short of labour before the war, and now had to compete with the growing military demands. However, military conscription meant compulsory labour, which suited the private employer. For example, men fled from the reserves to Rift Valley farms as squatters and unskilled labour. In February 1916, The *Leader of British East Africa*, a periodical, said: "There is more than enough labour freely offering for plantation work which is a great novelty for the cost."[9] The settler-dominated War Council secured the reduction of carrier wages to Rs.5 a week. The press approved, "We may almost regard the War Council as the Government," said the *East African Standard* in December 1915.[10]

Conscription could be used for blackmail. For example, Karen Blixen tells how her cook's former employer, the wife of a civil servant, threatened to have him conscripted if he did not come back to her. Esa, the cook, fled at dead of night, and only returned a year later after the war was over.[11] Conscription could also be used punitively. An employer who wanted to get rid of a servant, but could not prove that he had stolen something was told that the servant could be conscripted. On the other hand, the employer could refuse as evidenced by one Miss Buxton, who refused to allow a servant convicted of theft to go to the Carrier Corps;[12] and the DC Kisumu who considered sending a young and unsatisfactory headman to the Carrier Corps; and similarly, disposing of the undesirable retainers of Chief Onduso.[13]

Emigration into farms was less popular with government officers. In 1916, the Assistant District Commissioner Dagoretti gave two main reasons for it; escaping the rule of chiefs, and Carrier Corps impressment. District officers were well aware of the press-gang methods used by chiefs and their retainers to round up unwilling men. Commenting in 1917 on the problem of men moving from Murang'a District to Machakos, the DC stated the dilemma of District Officers and headmen with some heat:

> "Since veiled compulsion had to be used, was every headman to be deposed for every unjust act? Their successors would be ineffective and cause further attacks on government by the press. An officer over-zealous in preventing labour abuses ran the risk of being posted to some less pleasant district. Normal Leys, a government doctor noted for his outspokenness, was even sent to Nyasaland."[14]

The provincial administration depended entirely on chiefs, headmen and councils of elders. They raised labour, collected taxes, told District Officers what was going on and kept order. In the East Africa Protectorate, where there were no traditional chiefs, such men as Kinyanjui in Kiambu, Charier in Murang'a and Wambugu in Nyeri became chiefs and headmen because their abilities made them indispensable to the government. The Native Authority Ordinance of 1912 gave them greater authority to raise labour for government, and to recruit carriers when war came. Medals were given to those chiefs and headmen who had been particularly zealous in raising carriers, and in commandeering livestock to feed the troops.

Keeping on good terms with his people as well as with the

government demanded exceptional skill from a chief like that shown by Wambugu wa Mathangani from Nyeri. His services to government were appreciated so much for many years that he was awarded the War Medal. The Scots missionary doctor H.R.A. Philp was, however, very scornful of him. During the mass levy in 1917, hundreds of Wambugu's men bolted like rabbits in the dark before his eyes, and the DC had to confess that the great favourite had let the Government down.[15]

Was Wambugu really such a fool? Elijah Kaara of Mihuti, South Tetu, did not think so. As a clerk at the Nairobi Carrier Deport from 1914 to 1917, he had heard that Wambugu turned a blind eye if a recruit fled, especially if he had not been circumcised. Kaara told us,

> "I was able to save many Nyeri men by omitting their names. I would tell a man to carry a basket into the crowd and disappear. ... Wambugu was quite ... a tactful man. He was an intelligent man and he managed to keep his hands on everybody."[16]

This must have been tricky since his neighbours in Nyeri were both the DC and the PC. Fazan S.H., Wambugu's DC in 1929, noted that Wambugu was a much abler man in every way than one would have suspected on first acquaintance.

It is not surprising, then, that districts with strong headmen and councils fulfilled military demands most easily. This applied to most of Nyanza Province. Even in 1914-15, it produced over 18,000 carriers, 6,000 local military labour and 4,000 for the incessant military operations in Turkana, before the other three provinces had actually started. Most young Kalenjin joined the KAR or Nandi Scouts. They went into the Carrier Corps as syces and drivers only; never as carriers. As for the Maasai, they produced large numbers of livestock, but no men, except as scouts under Lord Delamere and other settlers. This must have given the moran plenty of excitement, with opportunities to raid across the border. An attempt to recruit members of the Purko section for the KAR failed after fourteen moran were shot when they attacked the troops sent to enforce the draft. This was the only time soldiers, as opposed to police or tribal retainers, were used for recruiting.

Nyanza was the largest recruiting area; but Seyidie is the most richly documented province of the four although it was the smallest. Its eleven files on "Porter Recruitment", together with many others, probably form the best carrier material anywhere. It was expected to supply a lot of first-line carriers in the belief that the Swahili porter tradition still survived. In 1915, however, an offer of Rs. 20 produced only three volunteers in Malindi, while a nocturnal press-gang produced another 200 whom the D.C., Mervyn Beech, described as "skallywags". Villagers now took to the bush if they saw an officer, actions that prompted the District Officer at Takaungu to say that a Swahili would work for an Arab, but disliked portage. He concluded that the safari tradition was in fact dead.

In February 1915, General Wapshare was trying to get gun porters and he finally achieved this with the help of Sheikh Ali bin Salim, Liwali of Mombasa, who paid his headmen 50 cents for each recruit. A staff officer said that they were of good class, but Hobley warned that as Muslims, they had to have preferential treatment over up-country men. Then 13 of them deserted: two Luos, three Kikuyus, a few coast men and some Nyamwezi from German East Africa. Two of these had been German askaris, and this caused some concern. General headquarters now asked for another 160 and at the same time

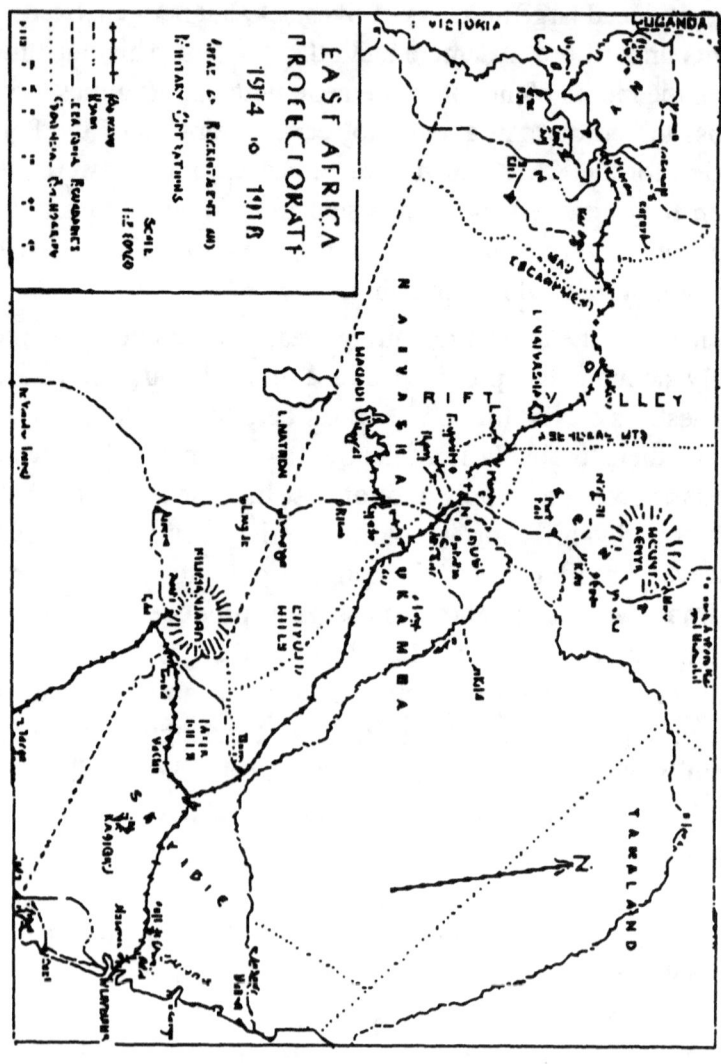

MAP 1: The East Africa Protectorate, 1914 to 1918: Areas of Recruitment and Military Operations

barred Kikuyus and men from German East Africa. When the demand was raised to 900, the PC Tanaland was approached, but only 160 locals were available in this sparsely populated province. The Pokomo were mostly canoemen, while the professional porters were Kikuyus. Beech said that he could get Kikuyu volunteers who had settled and had become more or less like coastmen. Therefore, Beech's statement provides some interesting evidence about pre-war population movements.

Beech also commented that to allow men to refuse service with impunity would most seriously have impaired the authority of the Liwali and headmen, to say nothing of his own. District Officers would unanimously have agreed with this comment. ,Probably the Native Followers Recruitment Ordinance of June 1915 took the pressure off Malindi by applying equal treatment for all. Recruiting was nevertheless, specially difficult among the Giriama and Duruma who had been sorely hit by what was called "the famine of the maize bags" in 1899. Their councils had been seriously weakened, and could not enforce their own or the government's will. Attempts to remedy this with closer administration caused the Giriama rising in August 1914.

The ever-increasing labour demands caused little trouble throughout the war. Of the two minor examples in 1914, the Giriama rising was due to pre-war administrative pressures. Afterwards, a fine was imposed of 1,000 porters for the Carrier Corps. In Kisii, there was a brief outbreak of looting set off by an unsuccessful German raid. In the first year, Ukamba produced very few carriers. The DC Machakos had feared that recruiting could cause trouble, which in fact never occurred. At first, the war looked like a game. Joseph Munyao (DC's clerk) and Mutiso Kanzivei (carrier) said that in Machakos they called it *Kau wa Mathyaka* (the war of the quivers). Said Munyao:

"*Anake* (young men) were collected and told to carry bows and arrows. This was how Kamba soldiers were called up before the British had been prepared."[17] Before the mass levy however, recruiting was usually done by a personal visit to each location in turn and an interview with the elders who, after the matter was put before them, usually supplied their quota of men. This was the recruiting method described by the DC Machakos in 1916.

Labour demands were often fulfilled with a readiness which attracted warm testimonials. For instance, the Provincial Commissioner Ukamba praised the loyalty of the population despite recruiting and commandeering. Though this might suggest that no very searching questions were asked as to how tribal authorities got results, there is no doubt that officers genuinely wished to refute accusations that the Africans were not pulling their weight in the war effort.

The unsupervised activities of headmen and their retainers tended to lead to illegality and violence, as the DC Murang'a noticed. Several war survivors also testified to the cruelty of headmen and retainers as the following examples show:

> "They were recruited by force and at least every house had to produce one young man. Their mothers were crying as they went," said Okech Atonga, a gun carrier from South Nyanza.[18]

> "The son of a man who was hated was taken. The son of a man who was respected was hidden by Kinyanjui wa Gatherimu. Ropes were put through their pierced ear lobes and tied together. This was a method often used by retainers," Leah Karuga, near Limuru, gave the women's point view.[19]

"Even before the mass levy, almost all had an intense fear and hatred of service in the Carrier Corps, but both chiefs and people had been loyal to the government and peacefully met demands for labour and stock," reported the DC Kisumu.[20]

Another method mentioned by Josphat Njoroge, of the Kikuyu Mission Volunteers, was of impounding the goats and possessions of defaulters.[21]

The survivors' testimonies were corroborated by Mr. Wahome Mutahi, *(Sunday Nation, 27th August 1989)* who wrote, "As a small boy, Gitahi Mehugu of Tetu saw the conscripts painfully secured by cords through their pierced ear lobes". Another person who corroborates the survivors' testimony is Elspeth Huxley in her novel *Red Strangers* which is based on oral field work done in Nyeri about 1931. In the novel, the fictitious chief "Muthengi", represents Mwirigo wa Irimu, described by his DC as "powerful, cunning and relentless as the enemy".[22]

Many deserted before reaching the depot in the field, or if overdue for discharge and near enough to home as happened to some Taitas. Watkins and Hobley (PC Seyidie) sympathised with them but felt that they had to be punished for what was a serious offence. Then of the 857 Dagoretti recruits, 168 deserted and only three were caught; the rest having hidden on farms or with friends. The appalling condition of repatriates and their grim tales naturally encouraged men to evade capture if they could. The DC Kitui reported in 1916 that people would flee when they heard that an officer was coming, and could not easily be reached in the empty lands towards the Tana River. In German East Africa, having already suffered German conscription, people would leave home and live near some isolated water-hole where game was plentiful. Dr. Philp tells this story:

> "After the first [conscription], Waitha fled and lived for the rest of the war on the banks of the Tana River, below Tumutumu Hill, coming out only to seek his food and scurry back."[23]

Wabunya wa Kihindo told us at Kabati Market that men would try to hide locally, rather than in the Tana or Athi valleys, as the risk of being caught on the way was too great. He escaped, but a friend who hid in a cave was caught.

In order to finish the campaign in 1917, the military wanted 160,000 carriers but they got about 120,000. John Ainsworth, PC Nyanza, was made Military Commissioner for Labour to organise this mass levy in the East Africa Protectorate, Uganda and the conquered German districts. He estimated from the tax registers how many men between 18 and 30 years of age were being medically rejected.

By about the end of May, all available labour in Seyidie had been rounded up. In Machakos, the councils were afraid of claims for blood money from the families of the dead, owing to the terrible mortality in the first six months of 1917, and the lamentable condition of repatriates returning home in May and June 1917. District Officers had to take charge. Mulei Nguyo, an askari who became a storekeeper stated:

> "Selection of the people was strict. A European came to a place called *Kwa Kithembe* on a horse, and the people were called out by name. They selected strong men, but not fat ones, who then walked to Nairobi."[24]

Raphael Osodo was a chief's clerk in Bunyala, the south-west corner of North Nyanza. The chief sent his retainers to arrest the young men, and Osodo recorded their names. As the war went on, the work increased, and he accompanied the askaris. He said that it was hard for a man to escape, because he had his name down and knew exactly where he came from. He mentioned a common fear that the white men ate conscripts. Some volunteered because they would have been conscripted anyway. Asembo Odera and Odandayo Agweli are two local men who joined 4th KAR for this reason.

Sometimes, deception was used as shown by Elspeth Huxley in her novel *Red Strangers*. She records that a big law case was to be held at Karatina, and everyone was to attend. Men were arrested and put into a huge wire cage' (also described by Dr. Philp). They were divided into three batches: Fita, Samba and Rotha. Fita went to Nairobi under escort. Samba, a small batch, worked on local European farms. Rotha, the old and infirm, were allowed to go home.

In Kisii, men were tricked into coming to the station ostensibly to cut grass, and were then recruited to the Carrier Corps. The seriousness of forced conscription came to the fore in 1938 when Hitler's aggressions in Europe aroused fears of war. Hardly anyone came to the Kisii sports, in case young men were conscripted again. However, the mass levy went on peacefully. Maybe by then, the people were too exhausted to protest. There were exceptions though. One was of fighting near Limuru in 1917, following raids on people living on the lands of the Uplands Bacon Factory. Subsequently, District Officers went through the hut tax lists with the elders, and men were enroled without trouble except in Nyika where a District Officer tried to recruit Giriama who had moved illegally into Malindi

District without notifying its DC. Unfortunately, a Giriama retainer fatally stabbed a Kauma elder.

To the relief of all, the mass levy was called off in August 1917. The DC Kiambu, G.A.S. Northcote, welcomed it for a most menacing atmosphere had been developing. Seyidie was still called for specialist workers of all kinds: motor drivers, grooms, blacksmiths, tailors, stevedores and even canoemen, who were now offered higher wages, as was the case in the first year of the war. Men were also wanted for the new military road which was being built from Kismayu to Serenli, to which rejects from the mass levy were sent. It became increasingly difficult to find labour in Mombasa.

The new DC Nyika stood up for the harassed Giriama. Hobley, PC Seyidie, asked in vain for the early repatriation of Taita who were working for the military railway department as there were no young men to clear the land for cereals or bananas. In German East Africa, British political officers protested angrily at the effects of recruiting sorely on people who had already been tried. Charles Dundas, formerly of the East Africa Protectorate, doubted if the official death lists were final and stated, "To judge by the human wrecks I have seen returning, I am convinced that numbers die after discharge".[25]

A leave scheme for carriers was abandoned because so many failed to return to duty. Repatriation was more important. At the end of the war, there were 64,622 men on the Military Labour Corps books. Longing for home could be fatal to a sick man, but so could a long journey. In June 1917, Ainsworth began to set up convalescent camps, at Mombasa, Voi, Nairobi and Kisumu. He staffed the camps with missionaries and other sympathetic people.

The camps reduced the political damage done by what the DC Machakos described as "the deplorable condition of discharged carriers who began to be repatriated in May and June [1917]." There is a harrowing scene in *Red Strangers* when the first men return: gaunt, dazed, bearded, and long-haired. They say, "We who have returned have sworn an oath never to speak of what we have seen."[26]

Apart from train and boat journeys, the road home was eased by ox-carts for the disabled, which Raphael Osodo remembered. The East African War Relief Fund, which Ainsworth had helped to start in 1915, provided extra cash. Most men walked home. For example, Mwova Kataka (carrier), and William Nthenge (stretcher bearer) walked from Athi River, while Okech Atonga (gun carrier) walked from Kisumu to Homa Bay. However, Asembo Odera, who had lost a leg with 4th KAR and was discharged at Bondo in Uganda, went to Kisumu by steamer, to Mumias by oxcart and was carried home by men detailed by the chief.

In that way, the survivors of the mass levy made their weary way home.

Carrier Logistics

We are the porters who carry the food, of the porters who carry the food of the porters who carry the food, etc.

According to Mr. H.B. Thomas, the above statement was a marching song current in Uganda soon after the return of the Baganda carriers from the advance to Tabora in 1916. It was devised by Dr. G.H. Hale Carpenter who had accompanied the force to Tabora. Nothing else could have shown more clearly the porters' shrewd and humorous understanding of the basic logistical problem than the above marching song. As the Watkins Report put it, a porter ate his own load in 25 days. His official load was 50 lbs and he needed 2 lbs of food a day. If he carried his own food and restocked at "Head" (the end of a line of communication), only half of his load would be available for other goods; if there were no goods at "Head", his load would consist only of his own food, and his journey was pointless, unless he could restock en route.

Under good conditions, porters could average twelve miles a day, taking fifteen days to reach "Head" on an average line of 180 miles long. On the 600 mile road from the Rhodesian railway to the German border, which was not under the Military Labour Bureau, porters carried 60 lbs for 15 miles a day, on nothing but 2 1/2 lbs of meal a day. This road was fairly level, whereas the Dodoma-Iringa line was very mountainous, and the Mikesse-Rufiji line notorious for its appalling swamping. Weather conditions could easily upset all these neat mathematical formulae.

In peacetime, government safaris took five days to carry meal from Nyeri to Meru from where it went on to Marsabit. If 100 loads of 60 lbs each were to be delivered in this time, 100 porters would be needed for the loads themselves, and twenty more for twenty loads to feed the food carriers and themselves. So 1,200 lbs extra was needed to get 6,000 lbs to Meru: 1,000 lbs for the porters who carried the food, and 200 lbs for the extra men, all at 2lbs per man per day. In this formula, x = the number of porters or loads:

$$X = 100 + \frac{(X \times 2lbs \times 5)}{60}$$

On the recommended Military Labour Bureau loading of 50 lbs, such a safari would have to be 125 strong in porters and loads. From Nyeri, these safaris were fed mainly en route as far as Meru. The lot of carriers like M'Kongo wa Maitai from Meru District must have had it rough. A porter had to carry his blanket, other belongings, a panga or jembe, or even a cooking pot, in addition to his official load.

This was known as the Convoy System, which was replaced in 1916 by the Dumping System in which a line had permanent posts every twelve miles or so, where labour was housed and fed. In very hilly country, posts were much closer together. A large amount of sifted meal was needed because coarse meal wasted transport as one pound out of six ended up being useless. It also took longer to cook and was harmful to health as it caused diarrhoea. The new system also ensured that mealie was properly cooked because to a tired man, raw mealie was poison. Thus, posts and dumping were vital to maintaining the health of both troops and carriers.

Each post had 50 labourers for building *bandas*, digging drains and latrines, and maintaining roads and bridges. On a line 180 miles long, 12,000 men needed 11,216 carriers and 750 post labour. The system was that 730 men would hand over their loads to an equal number at meeting place 0, midway between posts Nos. 14 and 15. The group returning down the line would take the sick and wounded. Loads would thus pass up the line, borne by falling numbers of carriers, up to meeting place *A*

Then 143 men would take loads over from a similar number from post No. 1. The labour force used over 500 loads of food a day which was over 25,000 lbs.

A Nigerian Battery Carrier, with a 70 lb. load, consisting of the wheel of a 2.95" mountain gun, its steel tyre being slung across his shoulder

from W.D. Downes, *With the Nigerians in German East Africa*

The War Strategy

leaving about 1,000 lbs in hand. A third of the men were reckoned to be off work each day. This comprised 4% headmen, 4% cooks, 10% sick, and 15% who were on their weekly rest day. In practice, this was never quite so for there was never enough labour. Fortunately, animal and mechanical transport assisted, thereby reducing the number of carriers needed on the Iringa and Rufiji Lines.

Until the British offensive in 1916, lines of communication based on the Uganda Railway were quite short; only those on the Kagera front in western Uganda were much longer. During the advance to the Central Railway, growing numbers of carriers were needed on the lines to Tabora, Morogoro and Dar es Salaam. We shall see how carriers predominated during the advances to the Rufiji and Iringa, and how the complicated operations in 1917 demanded more carriers than could in fact be supplied. However, although water, animal and mechanical transport played their part, the brunt was borne by the porters of the mass levy.

Means of transport and lines of communication

Many different types of transport were used especially in the early days of rapidly advancing columns. A carrier was supposed to take only 50 lbs, a donkey or ox 120 lbs, a mule about 200 lbs and a Ford light lorry 700 lbs including its driver and his kit. The role animals played is highlighted by Angus Buchanan of 25th Royal Fusiliers who describes the animal transport with the 1st Division, which advanced from Longido to Moshi in March 1916.

Buchanan describes a ponderous column of 4,000 fighting men which might have needed about 16,000 carriers. It found the country south of Kilimanjaro much too difficult, and arrived at Moshi too late to cut off the German retreat. On the march, such a column must have been many miles long). The ammunition wagons of the South African artillery were each drawn by a sixteen span of mules, driven by Cape Coloured men. The ammunition column at the rear consisted of two-wheeled carts, each drawn by two span of oxen and carrying 500 Ibs; the load of ten carriers. The Bishop of Zanzibar's carriers pulled these carts from Bagamoyo to Dar es Salaam, five men to each cart. By this time, most of the animals were dead. There were also four-wheeled wagons each carrying 3,000 to 4,000 lbs_ the load of seventy to eight carriers_ and drawn by ten span of mules, or sixteen to twenty span of oxen. A lot of syces and drivers were needed to look after these animals, a considerable number of which died of horse sickness and tsetse flies before the column reached Moshi. Its commander, Brigadier-General Stewart was blamed for the failure of the operation, but it seems clear that he had an impossible task.

Brigadier-General Northey's Nyasaland Field Force and its carriers were not under the East African Force. For them, there were two very long lines of communication. The first began with coastal steamers from Beira to Chinde in Portuguese East Africa, where river steamers took stores in barges to the railway at Chindio. After railage to Limbe, lorries carried goods to Lake Malawi, and after water transport to its head, carriers took over on lines which linked with the East African Force at Iringa.

The other line ran from the Rhodesian Railway north of Broken Hill to the German border, with a branch at Kasama to Abercorn and Fife. There is a unique official description of this line by Sir Lawrence Wallace, Administrator of North-Eastern Rhodesia. He reports that there was an alternative route with carrier transport at each end, between Ndola and Kasama and in the middle, there was a distance of 400 miles where goods were carried by canoes up the Luapula and Zambezi Rivers. These canoes could take between 120 Ibs and half a ton. They were propelled by a corps of 12,000 paddlers from the Bangweulu Swamps and adjacent rivers. The paddlers delivered 2,500 tons in over a year with little loss. Their recruitment was the result of skilful political work by District Officers among people with little experience of Europeans.

On the main road, the first method was to send a convoy of thirty ox wagons to the border with 100 tons of stores. The oxen would just make it before succumbing to tsetse flies. Ford cars then supplemented carriers on a hastily improved road; but on the round trip of 900 miles to Kasama, which was 150 miles short of the border and back, a car would use half of its 700 Ibs load of petrol. Thus, the logistical problem was the same with any form of transport which could not live off the country. For carriers, the route crossed a country which was sparsely inhabited. When food became scarce, difficulties increased rapidly as the route was through a country which could not feed the carriers at all, and the length of each section must have been less than that of a 12 day journey if anything at all was to be delivered.

If the 450 miles from the railway to Kasama was divided into five stages of seventy-five miles each, only one twenty-seventh of the original loads would actually have arrived with another 150 miles to the border. The logistics of delivering *only one ton of stores a day* was as follows:

Table 2: Logistics of Delivering One Ton of Stores a Day

At a distance of	with food on the road	with food also to be carried
150 miles	750 carriers	1,800 carriers
300 miles	1,500 carriers	7,150 carriers
450 miles	2,250 carriers	23,200 carriers
600 miles	3,000 carriers	71,000 carriers

The column needed *ten tons a day,* but for 350 miles of the line, food could usually be brought in. Only once did the whole line have to be fed from base. During the dry season, 40,000 carriers would be at work, and 20,000 or less during the rains. The loss of labour in the districts reduced their output of food. On both of these southern lines, much of the portage was seasonal. Men worked for a few months at a time from their homes, never going far away. Towards the end of the war, only a handful of these southern carriers were under the Military Labour Corps.

It is impossible to say how much of the stores carried were lost when animals or carriers collapsed and died, or when loads of food were soaked. During the heavy rains of late 1916 and early 1917 on the Rufiji and Iringa lines, losses of stores as well as of life were severe. For instance, in December 1916 the Senior Carrier Officer at Iringa protested at the treatment of his carriers by the 2nd Division. Rations were inadequate. Meal was not in waterproof bags and was being spoilt by the heavy rains. The report of a carrier officer, Captain Carnelly, will be described later to throw further light on the situation at Iringa.

It looks as though waterproof bags were becoming usual. They certainly were when the Kikuyu Mission Volunteers were at work on the Iringa line in September 1917. "We carried things like beans, sugar and dates in waterproof packets", said Kaniaru, a KMV man interviewed at Ngechu, Kiambu District.

The military need for carriers worked out at one, first, or second-line carrier for each rifle, with two more on the line of communication. Europeans needed more. The personal baggage allowance for an officer was 40lbs and 25lbs for an NCO. In practice, every man from officer to porter had little more than a blanket. An ideal allowance was 10lbs for a man, 20lbs for an officer, but no man could keep healthy on that scale for long.

Africans needed much less baggage than Europeans or Indians, but not less food in weight. European troops received rations which were, like those of Africans, far inferior to what they ate at home. In the field, it was tinned bully beef and biscuit. No wonder their health suffered. Only the most hardened whites - veteran KAR officers or others accustomed to life in the bush and used to shooting game - could really rough it. Angus Buchanan has much to say on this subject in *Three Years of War in East Africa*. In the Nigerian Brigade, where many of the officers were new to Africa, the allowance was two loads per European, and they were accordingly called the "bed and bath" brigade.[27] Weekly "chop boxes" came from Fortnum and Mason, a famous London delicatessen store, though presumably, they did less well during the hungry vigil on the Rufiji.

In a note to the Official Historian, Colonel Beazley remarked that von Lettow thought it foolish of the British to send raw young whites to fight in such a climate. Youngsters usually cracked up sooner than more mature men. Beazley was one of many who queried the whole policy of trying to conquer German East Africa at all, rather than to be content with just securing the Uganda Railway. He concluded, "[Kitchener] seems to have been right", a conclusion which would seem to be confirmed by the vast efforts demanded of carrier transport.[28] The war would after all be won in Europe, not in East Africa.

Notes

[1] Horden, *Operations in East Africa*, Appendix 2.
[2] von Lettow, *Reminiscences*, 8-9 and 22.
[3] Meinertzhagen, *Army Diary,* 83-84.
[4] von Lettow, *Reminiscences*, 3-4 and 29.
[5] Meinertzhagen, *Army Diary*, 164, 186.
[6] Moyse-Bartlett, KAR 152-159.
[7] Watkins, *Report,* Paragraph 50.
[8] von Lettow, *Reminiscences*, 3-4 and 29.
[9] *Leader*, 5 Feb, 1916, "Labour and Discipline".
[10] *East African Standard*, 3 Dec. 1915, and *Leader*, 6 Nov. 1915.
[11] Blixen, *Out of Africa*, 242.
[12] Watkins Papers, C.M. Dobbs (DC) to Ainsworth, 14, Aug. 1916.
[13] Kenya National Archives, DC/CN7/1, DC to DC. 25 Oct. and 25 Dec. 1915.
[14] Kenya National Archives, PC/CP6/3/1, "Emigration From the Reserves 1917", Ross, *Kenya*, 280, refers to three transfers including that of Leys: Norman Leys, *Kenya* (London: 4th ed., Cass, 1973), 152 mentions a District Officer who shot himself after such a transfer
[15] Philp, *God and the African*, 108-112.
[16] Kenya National Archives, DC/NYERI/6/1. Nyeri PRBI, 8 Sept. 19129.
[17] Extract from interview with Joseph Munyao, 1965, kindly given by Dr. J. Forbes Munro.
[18] Notes kindly given by Richard Siaga, 26 Aug. 1970.
[19] The method of securing young men was seen by C. Dundas. *African Crossroads,* (London: MacMillan, 1955). 19; it is mentioned by Marius Karatu and in notes of interview kindly given by James Karuga, Thomsons Falls.
[20] Kenya National Archives, DC/CN1/5/1, AR 1916-1917.
[21] The method of securing young men was seen by C. Dundas. *African Crossroads* (London: MacMillan, 1955), 19, it is mentioned by Marius Karatu and in notes of interview kindly given by James Karuga, Thomsons Falls.

22 Huxley, *Red Strangers*, 272-273; Philp, "The Wire Cage" in *Kikuyu News*, No. 66, (Feb.-Apr. 1918), 8-10. I am told by Mr. John Johnson, once District Officer at Kerugoya, Embu District, that this was the name of the circumcision group for 1917; in Meru it was apparently *Kaaria* - see oral source (Meru District) for M'Inoti and Muthanya.

23 H.R.A. Philp, *God and the African in Kenya* (London: Marshall, Morgan and Scott, n.d.), 131.

24 Notes kindly given by Philip Mwalali, Kiteta, 1969.

25 Watkins papers, Byatt to Deputy Adjutant and Quartermaster General, Nov. 1917, and enclosures.

26 Huxley, *Red Strangers*, 278-282.

27 Downes, *Nigerians*, 55; Public Records Office, Cabinet Office Papers 45/30B, as quoted. Von Lettow, *Reminiscences*.

28 Philp Magnus, *Kitchener: Portrait of an Imperialist* (London: Murray, 1958), 283-288, 380.

Chapter Three

In the Battlefields

Defending the Uganda Railway: 1914-1915

Ngeretha na Geremani niithui Mwaruagira? English and Germans, were you fighting for us? (Kikuyu song, quoted by Leah Karuga)

The outbreak of war was followed by a flush of patriotic enthusiasm in East Africa. Settlers flocked into Nairobi and a rash of irregular settler units appeared; the only one of any permanent importance being the East African Mounted Rifles. Many of its members were to fall on *3rd November* at Longido, on the German side of the border and on the road to Arusha. An unavoidable British defeat was the German occupation of Taveta from where the Assistant DC, S.H. La Fontaine, withdrew with his men.[1]

Fighting erupted on several minor fronts which included Lakes Victoria, Tanganyika and Malawi. The British gradually won control of all the three Lake fronts by a series of mini-naval victories. In the West of Lake Victoria, there were clashes in Kagera, where co-operation with the Belgians was necessary. Abercorn in North-Eastern Rhodesia was held by a handful of police loyally supported by villagers and convicts who carried water, machine-guns and ammunition. The loss of African lives in a sharp action at Karonga, near the head of Lake Malawi, contributed to the rising of John Chilembwe, a Christian pastor trained in the USA, who made perhaps the only articulate protest against African involvement in the war. He and his followers took to arms with inevitable and tragic results.²

In these area, the numbers involved were small while the distances were great. Two long lines of communication were opened by the British, both involving many thousands of carriers and canoemen. One ran about 600 miles from the Rhodesian railhead near Broken Hill (Kabwe) to the German border. The other used river, rail, road and lake transport to the northern end of lake Malawi where carriers took over up to the border.

By far, the most important front was the northern one behind which ran the vital and vulnerable Uganda Railway. Ignoring von Schnee's orders, von Lettow concentrated on Moshi where he planned to attack the railway and invade Voi or Mombasa, while keeping the British firmly on the defensive for over a year.

The East African Force had its headquarters in Nairobi. Its first commander was Major-General Wapshare, not a fighting man but a competent administrator who laid the foundations for the 1916 offensive. The British had the following four areas of operations in the East Africa Protectorate for which they recruited African labour:- The first, and the most important, was based at Voi where the main road to Taveta was joined by another running from Tsavo station via Mzima Springs. The second area was along the coast road from Mombasa to the border at Vanga; by then, the Germans had reached Gazi, only thirty miles from Mombasa. The third was on the road to Namanga, 100 miles from Nairobi while the fourth was between Kisumu and the border. In September, a German attempt to attack the railway viaducts was defeated at Kisii as their carriers panicked and the British resistance became too strong.

The first three areas of operation covered the vulnerable railway stretch from Maji Chumvi (48 miles from Mombasa) to Kiu, 250 miles. In over a year, fifty-six attacks were made on the railway by the Germans, ten being between July and November 1915, and within Voi District alone. This was a heroic achievement by the German patrols, but they never succeeded in closing the railway for long. The raids were certainly a nervous strain on all concerned thereby prompting an Indian stationmaster to remark: "A collision, there you are! An explosion, where are you?" A train carrying General Tighe, Wapshare's successor, was also attacked but the damage was quickly repaired though the railway's carrying capacity was reduced as it became impossible to run trains at night. Morale, bad enough after Tanga, was kept low as the British felt that the Germans under von Lettow could run rings around them.

Wapshare was replaced in April 1915 by Major-General Tighe, who was a good fighting man, but not clever enough for the political side of his duties. Then Brigadier-General Stewart was sent to attack Bukoba, the German port on Lake Victoria. Although he succeeded in destroying the wireless station, he handled the operation badly and it ended with a disgraceful orgy of plunder. Tighe should have made a better job of this operation which was the only successful one during his term of office.

Von Lettow's reputation as commander, leader, administrator and improviser has stood the test of time. He was finally to surrender, undefeated, after the armistice in 1918. The first two British commanders-in-chief, Wapshare and Tighe, failed to concentrate their forces; they left isolated posts to be captured by the enemy, and had no proper reserve of troops. Discipline was bad at all levels as both generals tended to accept advice from officers of dubious ability and from certain settlers; advice which was both wrong and biased. Relations with the government and settlers in the East Africa Protectorate remained poor throughout the campaign.[3]

There were three extenuating circumstances though. First, von Lettow's force enjoyed internal communications unlike the British whose troops were of very uneven quality and low morale - the Germans also excelled at patrol work as opposed to the British troops which relied only on the KAR. Secondly, the British built new roads from Mombasa to Msambweni and from Tsavo past Mzima to Maktau. They also built the military railway from Voi through Maktau towards Taveta with a water pipeline across the Serengeti plain in Tsavo. These impressive works were all made possible by African labour and were the foundation for the 1916 offensive. Thirdly, Wapshare had little help from Kitchener who was infuriated by the Jasin disaster in January 1915. Jasin, a fort on the coast across the German border, had been taken by the British but von Lettow recaptured it with its full garrison. Kitchener told Wapshare that offensive operations were unnecessary. As War Minister, Kitchener refused to delegate despite his professed belief in staff work. He would neither allow the General Staff to shape strategy, nor share responsibility for the vast recruiting drive and for war industry. His legendary reputation faltered after the Dardanelles disaster in 1915.

The British were slow to win naval supremacy in the Indian Ocean as the Germans proved to be more organized than them.

For example, the German light cruiser *Konigsberg*, a fast new ship armed with 105mm guns, outclassed the old British cruisers. (A lasting reminder of this are guns from both the *Konigsberg* and her victim, HMS *Pegasus*, which can still be seen outside Fort Jesus at Mombasa, Kenya). The *Konigsberg* was finally cornered in the Rufiji Delta, where she was sunk on 11th July 1915 in a dangerous operation carried out by two monitors and shallow draft vessels with six inch guns. Their fire was directed by aerial observation, in an early use of a revolutionary technique. Unfortunately, the British navy failed to ensure that the *Konigsberg's* guns were destroyed thereby enabling the Germans to salvage ten 105mm and two 88mm guns and converting them into better field pieces than anything the British had. These guns were superior to the eight old four inch guns which the British recovered from the sunken *Pegasus*. Later, the crew of the *Konigsberg* formed an infantry company but their fate was tragic since about half were killed in one ambush.[4]

The German forces received another boost due to negligence by British naval vessels in that they recovered most of their cargo from the German blockade runner, the *Rubens or Kronborg* which was sunk in Mansa Bay near Tanga. The cargo recovered was: two 60mm field guns, 7,500 artillery shells of all necessary sizes, six machine-guns, 1,800 rifles, 3,000,000 rounds of ammunition, and other vital supplies. Von Lettow called it the biggest British mistake of all for without the recovered cargo, he might as well have had to give up. It is worthy mentioning however that the salvage of the *Rubens* cargo and *Konigsberg* guns was made possible by the labour of thousands of Africans enlisted on the German side.

The blockade of the Germans by the British navy was ineffective because of its incompetence and bad relations with the army. However, the British defeats at Tanga, Jasin and Longido were somewhat redeemed by modest successes at Kisii, Keronga and Abercorn. Even if von Lettow could not be everywhere at once, it is noteworthy that British detachments of African troops and police seemed to have had the better of the various minor but fierce engagements which took place in the remote areas near the Lakes and on the Rhodesian border. But after Jasin, von Lettow had everything his own way. He was in control, invading the East Africa Protectorate and attacking the railway at will. The overdue evacuation of outlying posts led to the defeat of a column at Salaita Hill, seven miles east of Taveta in March. There were equal numbers of soldiers and carriers, 158 of them and 98 donkeys. In this battle, British machine-gun carriers panicked. Ironically, the Germans were later to suffer a similar embarrassment at Mbuyuni.

When the new railway reached Maktau in June, it invited more German attacks. Wapshare persuaded Kitchener to raise two more battalions of KAR whose superiority to most Indian troops was now clear to all but the most blinkered. A senior staff officer, Colonel Sheppard, wrote that the KAR hardly ever lost a rifle; that only the most highly trained troops were a match for them. Nevertheless, the KAR had rivals at patrol work who were: Wavell's Arab Rifles, intelligence agents and armed scouts like Meinertzhagen's Drought's Skin Corps, and the Nandi scouts. Wavell was a regular officer who had been to Mecca and had a genius for leading Muslims. His death with many of his men in an engagement in Gazi District meant the end of the Arab Rifles.

In this summary of military operations, the dependence of Europeans on African labour has been emphasised: in the front line, in load-carrying, in unloading ships and in engineering works of all kinds. The military turned at once for labour to the civil authorities of the East African colonies. Undoubtedly, German East Africa and the East Africa Protectorate were the best organized colonies to meet this need. The East African Carrier Corps unit was thus born.

The unit was started by a District Commissioner, named Oscar Ferris Watkins. He left Oxford University to serve in the Boer War. Then he worked in the South African Mounted Police, and later as a municipal clerk in Pretoria. Here, he learned the value of finger-printing in identifying illiterate people which was to be the bedrock of Carrier Corps administration. He came to the East Africa Protectorate in 1908 as a District Officer. On his first leave in 1912, he returned to Oxford University to study for a Diploma in Anthropology in which he passed with distinction. He contributed articles to various learned journals which, with his exceptional command of Swahili, led to his appointment to lead the Carrier Corps.[5]

In August 1914, Watkins and another District Officer, J.M. Pearson, went to Mombasa to organise carriers for *B* force whose whereabouts was still unknown. Some of these men were used for the military operations which followed the recent rising in Giriama District against closer administration. One of the penalties imposed on the Giriama was a "fine" of 1,000 porters. Hundreds of men poured in from the three up-country provinces of the East Africa Protectorate which, with Seyidie, provided carriers throughout the war: Nyanza, Ukambani (including Kiambu) and Kenia (with an "i"); Murang'a, Nyeri,

K.A.R. askari with a Vickers heavy machine gun
Courtesy of Dr. Clive Irvine

Embu and Meru. The headman of each batch would be given a list by his D.C. Another 1,000 men arrived from Uganda under two District Officers, one of whom, E. L. Scott, had had experience in rationing labour during the building of the Busoga Railway. He became one of Watkins' most trusted advisers.

Five individual Carrier Corps were formed each comprising two officers, a medical officer, a corps headman and about 1,000 men, divided into ten companies under two or three headmen. The officers were soon given military ranks, Watkins becoming a captain and the others lieutenants. Unlike the German field companies, British units had no permanent carriers. Military officers tended to take men without reference to carrier headquarters. The result was increased administrative confusion, already caused by men deserting and joining friends in *C* force, so that the district lists soon became useless. Consequently, men would lose pay and worse still the protection of their own officers who were responsible for their diet and health. This was the basic reason for the terrible mortality which ensued.

Watkins at once saw the need to retain control. As early as October 1914, he clashed with Pearson over this issue. Pearson had obeyed an order from a staff officer at Mombasa to move the Carrier Corps No.1 from Mazeras to Gazi without referring the order to Watkins. Consequently, Pearson resigned. The highest rank Watkins ever reached was Lieutenant-Colonel, which gave him insufficient authority to prevent military officers interfering with his men. Watkins always put his civil duty first when the rights of carriers were endangered.

After Tanga, the unlucky carriers from *B* force disembarked at Mombasa after considerable sufferings in open lighters. They merged with *C* force carriers most of whom were syces and mule drivers and had already joined units. Then the Uganda carriers returned home at the end of the year after shocking losses from disease. Afterwards, the East Africa Carrier Corps was disbanded and Uganda and the East Africa Protectorate were given separate Transport Corps, each with its carrier section. Watkins was in charge of the East African Transport Carrier section.

Gazi became the most active area following the disaster at Jasin, up to April 1915 when the Voi Military Railway begun. The carriers were hard at work on the new road from Mombasa to Msambweni, through the malarious coastal belt which was unhealthy both for Europeans and for up-country Africans. Watkins could have preferred local men working from their own home as was being done successfully in Voi, Nyasaland, and Rhodesia. There, locally based men were being fed at home without having to acclimatize, a lesson which war experience drove home.

The military authorities in Voi and Gazi conceded that though up-country men might be less likely to desert, they were more likely to die in an unfamiliar climate. This was so because alarm was growing about the sickness and death among carriers on the coast by August 1915, especially among the Kikuyu. Charles Dundas, D.C. Mombasa, and G.H. Osborne, D.C. Gazi, advised that since the Digo people had recently suffered from the German invasion, it would make good political sense to use Digo carriers locally under their own headmen and exempt them from other service.

Watkins was always a civil officer in outlook and sensitive to political considerations. Just as von Schnee was at odds with von Lettow, so relations were always frigid between Watkins and his immediate superior, Brigadier-General C. P. Fendall, Deputy Adjutant and Quartermaster-General. Fendall was not an easy man to work with as evidenced by his private diary which contained extremely intolerant opinions of others including that of Watkins. He was unsympathetic about Watkins' political scruples, but had to admit that Watkins' government held him responsible for the welfare of his men. The strain of war increased the friction between civil and military officers who were gradually forced to realise that neglecting the health of their followers was not only inhuman, but also impaired the efficiency of the fighting troops.

Authority of the carrier section was frequently flouted by officers of local units. For example, in February 1915, Watkins sent Carrier Corps No. 6 to Msambweni, followed by another 238 whose return he requested in March, only to be told that the Royal Engineer officer in charge was reluctant to release them for another week because they knew their work. This was reasonable enough but Watkins was angered at the officer's successful appeal to General Wapshare behind his back.

In April 1915, supplies and transport sections at Kajiado sent a telegram to carriers at Mombasa saying: "I cannot spare porters, all engaged on vegetable gardens." Watkins' note to Major Neave, Assistant Director of Transport, Nairobi, runs:

> "Can we be of any further assistance to this gentleman? A flower garden would improve his camp, and a laundry would no doubt be useful. One might add stock farming to market gardening and secure his meat supply."[6]

Neave replied stiffly that attempts at facetiousness were not desirable in official correspondence. That Watkins did not appear to know that growing vegetables for the troops was one of the duties of the supplies and transport corps at Kajiado. In such a case, supplies should have raised their own labour, and not helped themselves to men for whose welfare the carrier section was responsible. All this goes to show how ill-defined the status of a military follower was. There was a long way to go before the point of view of the Carrier Corps staff was accepted.

Preparing to attack: 1915-1916

Donkeys were also used for carrying loads, but they were left well to the rear, lest the enemy hear the noise they make, and know the exact position of our troops
(Silvano Mutiso Mwoloi, medical orderly, Mukaa, Machakos District)

It is misleading to think that for the first eighteen months of the war, there was no thought of anything but defending the Uganda Railway. Morale had to be restored, so preparations were made for an offensive based on Voi, as the 1897 scheme had foreseen. Vital engineering works were needed. It fell mainly to the men of Voi District, especially those from the Taita Hills, to build the new cart track from Voi to Maktau, the road from Tsavo station to Mzima and Maktau, the military railway, and the water pipeline from the Bura Hills. The railway construction was under two engineers from India, Sir William Johns and Colonel Sutherland, who had originally come with *B* force. The labour included Indian Army Sappers and Miners, coolies, and 2,000 Taitas recruited by La Fontaine who was formerly, the Assistant D.C. Taveta.

Construction work often varied by active operations. Watkins records that a Carrier Corps might be a flying column one day, and split into small gangs along a section of railway line on the next. That control became very difficult, as an enemy attack on a post usually meant the dispersal into the bush of every unarmed African, who often seized the moment to desert ... to join friends at some other post or offer himself as a personal servant to some officer or NCO passing on column.

The Carrier Section was neither responsible for permanent railway labour, nor for those on the pipeline. It was only responsible for the Maktau road and the road from Mzima to Maktau. The Carriers were under the East Africa Pioneers who did not treat them well. One of their headmen complained to W.A. F. Platts, the D.C. Voi, who noted that the headman had been beaten by the Pioneers, presumably for his impertinence in reporting the state of affairs to him. A Royal Engineers officer blamed the Pioneers for keeping the men over their three months contract. There was also desertion from one unit to another if men became dissatisfied with the conditions. Another independent group was the 1,500 strong African Labour Corps. All non-combatants were merged with the carrier section in February 1916 to form the Military Labour Bureau. Military railways, however, remained a separate organisation and kept the Taita men who had become experts in railway work.

Animals proved an unreliable substitute for carriers. It was proposed that a batch of 350 donkeys be sent to help out on the Msambweni road, but they were recuperating at Machakos, perhaps after service on the Namanga road. Animals were used wherever possible, even in tsetse-fly country, until they died. Among the animals were: mules, horses, oxen, donkeys and even camels in about that order of usefulness. By December 1914. many beasts of burden had died from tsetse in Voi District.

including camels, which seem not to have been used again. General Wapshare described the problems as follows:

> Porters are very expensive and are never dependable, whilst water precludes their use for large bodies of troops. The supply of oxen is not plentiful, and it will damage the country considerably if large numbers are taken for military purposes. It would greatly increase our chances of success if India could earmark a mule corps for use in B.E.A. when the general offensive is resumed after the building of the railway."[7]

Wapshare noted that donkeys were easier to get than mules, but were only a makeshift since they were noisy and hard to control and carried only half the weight of a mule. They were unsuited for active operations as exemplified by one occasion in the Tsavo area when a braying donkey betrayed a patrol to the enemy. One mule could carry 2,000 rounds of .303 ammunition, a donkey or ox 1,500, and a porter 500. It could carry the barrel and tripod of a heavy machine-gun, and one box of ammunition each of which would require one carrier. Two mules could therefore take the load of three donkeys, or eight porters.

Tsetse fly was a lethal danger to animals; and even though the open Serengeti between Maktau and Taveta was relatively free of it, the fly occurred in bushes up to about 3,500 feet. The Namanga road crosses a country which is high enough to be free of tsetse and suitable for ox-carts. Marius Ng'ang'a Karatu, later a political activist in Limuru, worked on this road with ox-carts provided by the Roman Catholic Bishop. The Germans surrounded his detachment and burnt their carts, but Karatu made his way to Nairobi on a bicycle which he had the forethought to bring with him.

Syces, grooms and drivers were skilled followers who were much in demand. Nguku Mulwa of Muthetheni, east of Machakos, started as a stretcher bearer but later became a mule driver. But even with the short lines of communication which existed before February 1916, there were never enough porters, which in Wapshare's opinion, was partly due to the grave tension then existing between the Indian Headquarters and the local inhabitants, black and white. Other reasons were disease, administrative problems, desertion, poor distribution and wasteful use of manpower. In Uganda, for example, there was an instance of five carriers being allocated to each sepoy of the 13th Rajputs, though one could not imagine this being allowed in Voi or Gazi. Labour still had to be provided for private or government needs, including the military operations in Turkana, Jubaland and Marsabit.

For the first year of the war, the pre-war system of partly voluntary recruitment was used to raise carriers. Military service soon proved unpopular, despite monthly pay rates which often exceeded the four or five rupees with *posho* (rations) usually for unskilled labour. For once, the General Staff and the settlers were in agreement that a pay of Rs. 15 or 20 was too much.

Until September 1915, the prevailing mood among officials and settlers had been "business as usual" strongly endorsed by the Governor, Sir Henry Belfield. Officials even went on leave as if it was peace time. The big change came with the mass meeting at the Theatre Royal in Nairobi on 8th September 1915, when settlers, led by Ewart Grogan, demanded universal conscription. One result was the Native Followers Recruitment Ordinance, under which carriers for the 1916 operations were to be recruited.

It must not be thought that the government had done nothing towards the war effort. District Officers had been recruiting military labour, maintaining political control and, in districts adjacent to German East Africa, organising an intelligence service and risking their own lives on patrols. The P.C. Mombasa, C.W. Hobley, had to demand that his officers in Gazi, Rabai and Voi be given military ranks and the right to wear uniforms in order to prevent them from being shot if they were captured by the Germans.

The Central Committee of Supply and its branches started in 1914, was made up of both officials and settlers with the duty of controlling foodstuffs and other vital supplies. They had laid down the law to the Carrier Corps over the quality of meal, refusing to admit that it could be a cause of disease. The Theatre Royal meeting was followed by the setting up of the War Council, which further enhanced settler power, especially when it lowered the basic carrier pay from Rs.10 to Rs.5 a month.

Conscription also involved Europeans and Asians. The carrier section needed European staff, preferably local men who knew something on the men they would lead and spoke Swahili, knowledge which was fundamental, but too often lacking. For example, a Hindustani-speaking officer who had been transferred elsewhere when the Carrier Section was formed was later returned, to Watkins' annoyance. South Africans did not know Swahili and were then quite useless at first.

Watkins was quite often given men who were totally unsuitable without prior consultation. He made his position clear:

> "I can only use two kinds of Europeans, the young and active man who can march with a transport column, and the trained office man for depot work ....

> I cannot carry on if my staff are chosen for me from the point of view of their needs rather than mine."[8]

There was an unseemly row between an Indian army medical officer and a carrier corporal, in private life, a plantation manager, who then resigned. Perhaps the Indian had been officious towards a racially biased European. While not condoning the corporal's behaviour, Watkins told the Senior M.O: "The indiscretion of one of your staff has added to my difficulties, which in the matter of staff are already considerable".[9] There was for example, a Cape Town barrister who applied for a commission which he appeared to consider due to himself as a right, a view which Watkins did not share. Another one was unpopular with his colleagues but belonged to that class of men who appears always to be at work and at the end of the day has nothing to show for it.

One could find a constant triangle of contention with settlers, officials and Indian Army staff, all eyeing each other suspiciously. Settlers and Army staff could be seen ganging up against officials over pay and rations for African labour. This is confirmed in a letter from Watkins to H. R. McClue, D.C. Nyeri:

> "Labour has been thrown out to military officers, who can't understand what it says and don't know what it eats or where to get its food. In India, they say, a native can always feed himself ... they continue to distribute the porters in details of 50 to 100 and expect us to supervise them all. The men you mention were not mine, but thanks for the information. It may make a lever for moving the Indian Army."[10]

The payment of discharged carriers was to be a constant source of trouble, arising from the inaccuracy of the original registers which were passed on by the old carrier corps to the carrier section. Improvisation had been inevitable at the start in order to set up a system of nominal rolls and identification so that men could be paid. This is shown by an exchange of letters between Watkins and another D.C. with whom his relations may already have been cool. Watkins disliked the tone of the D.C.'s remarks about the pay sheets, which returning carriers were supposed to give to their D.C.s, who could then pay the men off promptly. This incident in February 1915 shows that carriers were only serving for up to six months, and raise a recurring but unanswerable question: how far were statistics falsified by plural recruitments?

It was an unhappy situation. An Indian Army staff had been thrown at short notice into an African territory, and was expected to work with its government, settlers and people. One of the forces under it had been shamefully defeated at Tanga. Confidence could hardly be inspired by the lack of proper planning before the war by the offices concerned, namely, the War, Colonial and India Offices, and their inability to act in harmony even when war had broken out. Political officers in East Africa could be pardoned for feeling that they were expected to fill a gap left open by the War Office and the Government of India.

Of the four provinces where carriers were recruited, only Seyidie was a theatre of war. Not only was there conscription, but also enemy invasion. People were subjected to intimidation from both sides, and in Gazi, there were reports of German atrocities not only by askari but also by Europeans. The British shot men suspected of aiding the enemy, and after the fall of their post at the isolated hill of Kasigau, three men were shot, six imprisoned, and the rest of the community deported to Malindi due to the incompetence of its commander. The D.C. Voi was highly critical of this military punishment but he praised the attitude of the Taita towards the government. It is a familiar story of suffering which is the inevitable consequence of war on its defenseless victims, whatever its professed aims.

The British were fortunate in their relations with the Arab ruling class on the coast. They relied on them for recruiting, intelligence and for the general support of the public. The exception was the Mazrui clan who had never accepted the rule of Zanzibar. The sons of Mbaruk, leader of the 1895 rising, stirred up some disaffection against the British, and were alleged to have encouraged the Giriama rising but the British had no reason to worry about Arab loyalty. The Germans found that their alliance with the Sultan of Turkey made them unpopular in the East, especially after the beginning of the Arab revolt against the Turks in the Hejaz.

Hence, the first eighteen months of the East African war was not a happy time for the British, and even less so for the people of the East Africa Protectorate. Furthermore, the expulsion of the Germans did not mean an end to their sufferings.

The Smuts offensive: 1916

We said if God kept us we would go home, for we knew that one does not die unless by the will of God

(Nguku Mulwa, stretcher bearer and mule driver)

The year 1915 ended with the appointment of two generals to take the offensive in the new year. Brigadier-General Edward

In the Battlefields

Northey was to command the southern forces in Nyasaland and North-Eastern Rhodesia. Sir Horace Smith-Dorrien, a distinguished officer whose experience went back to the Zulu War of 1879, and the British defeat at Isandlwana, was to command the East African Force. Meinertzhagen's reaction was that Smith-Dorrien would stop the rot, but he was wrong if he thought that he could bring von Lettow to terms; the cost in casualties and money would be high. Forty years later, the historian of the KAR agreed that the whole situation was thought out in terms of guns, aeroplanes and lorries, instead of bushcraft, carriers and quinine.

An offensive was now possible, thanks to the engineering works and to those who had built them. The plan was adopted by the cabinet despite Kitchener's protests. He grudged the extra manpower and materials which would be needed at the expense of the new volunteer armies on the Western Front.

Smith-Dorrien reached Cape Town too ill to continue. He was replaced by General Smuts, who with General Botha had beaten the nationalist rebels in 1914 and had then conquered German South-West Africa. This appointment was politically attractive in both Cape Town and London. The South Africans had the manpower, and were confident that they could soon repeat their success in South-West Africa. Actually, some of them thought that they would be allowed to keep German East Africa after the war. A rapid conquest would be good for the morale of the British public after the costly disasters of 1915.

South African troops had arrived ahead of Smuts, but on 12th February 1916, they were blooded in yet another unsuccessful attempt by Tighe to take Salaita Hill which commanded the road to Taveta. It was a chastening experience for them, both in the difficulties of bush warfare, and in the prowess of German askaris and of crack Indian troops like the Baluchis. Having held their ground against German attacks, the Baluchis returned to loot the machine-guns which South Africans had abandoned. The arrival of Rhodesian and more Indian troops meant that the overdue expansion of the KAR had again been postponed.

Smuts loved the traditional Boer method of manoeuvring the enemy out of his position rather than costly assaults. He had much to learn.

> "Smuts underrates the fighting qualities of the German native soldier", wrote Meinertzhagen. "I told him that in the bush he would find them as good as his South Africans... we spoke also about malaria and the dense bush which von Lettow likes for his manoeuvres. Smuts dislikes bush; he will like it less in a year's time."[11]

Military operations in any war depend unglamorously upon supply and transport. In the East African campaign, the dependence on carriers increased relentlessly as lines of communication lengthened. The carrier section had to change with the times. The capture of the post at Kasigau by the Germans increased the threat to the railway along which carriers became so spread out that the system of large corps collapsed. It was replaced by a more flexible system of gangs of about twenty-five men, each under a headman and preferably of the same tribe; but even gangs could be split up and control lost. Furthermore, by 1916, the carrier section was not only concerned with transport, but also with construction workers and all other kinds of labour.

In February 1916, the Military Labour Bureau was set up with

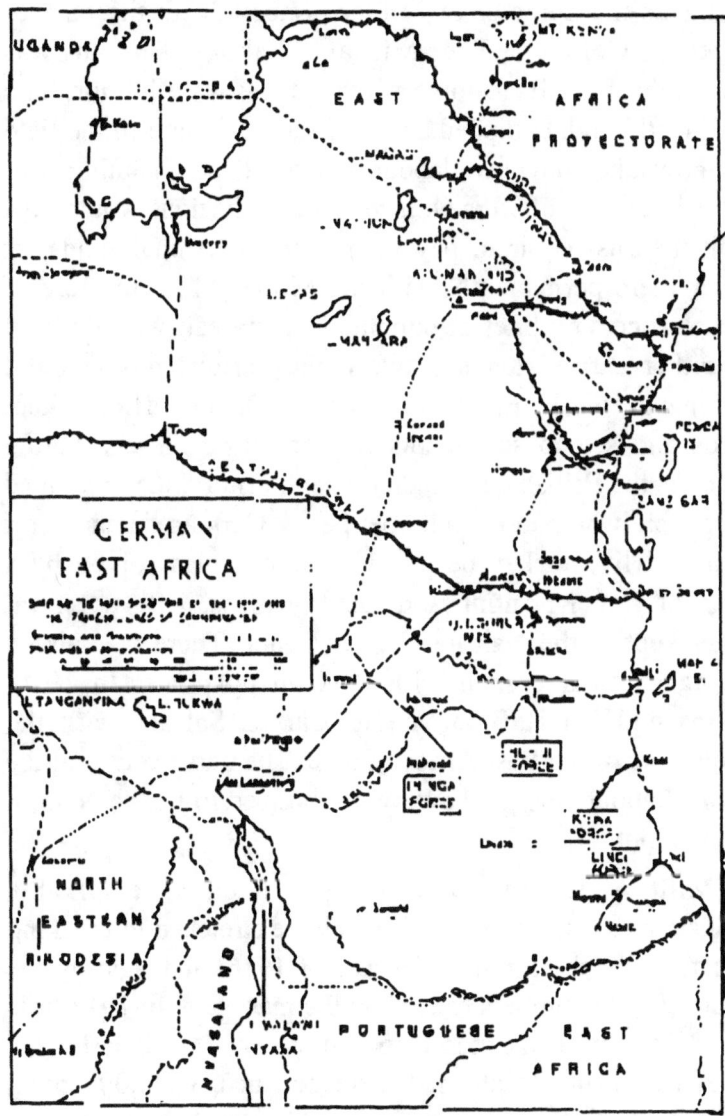

MAP 2: German East Africa showing the main operations of 1914-1917. and the principle lines of communication

Watkins as the Director of Military Labour with the rank of Lieutenant-Colonel. The Military Labour Bureau was responsible for all followers except railway labour, and subsequently both equipped and paid them. No unit in the field could now take on its own labour because it had no authority to pay them. Labour officers with advancing divisions would now recruit men as required, pay them from divisional funds, or register them permanently with the Military Labour Bureau. Labour officers on lines of communication dealt with the men who either carried loads between the various posts or did maintenance work. Finally, Advanced Depot Officers kept records and set up sub-depots for recruiting or repatriating labour. As the British occupied German territory, they recruited from people who had already met heavy German demands for labour and livestock. The problem of pay was solved by a system of finger-printing and identity discs, with a central register kept at the Nairobi Carrier Depot. There was also a growing medical branch with its own hospitals. In 1916, Watkins and his staff moved to Dar es Salaam with the headquarters of the East African Force. The nerve centre of the Military Labour Bureau, however, continued to be the Nairobi Carrier Depot.

The Military Labour Bureau represented a remarkable administrative feat, but its resources were stretched to breaking point; first, by the Smuts offensive of 1916, and then by the vast increase in numbers caused by the mass levy in 1917. It is not certain how many men it took over. By March 1916, the East Africa Protectorate had produced nearly 72,000 men, perhaps a third of whom went to the Military Labour Bureau. In April 1916, Smuts had 30,000 carriers. Before his advance began, carriers used to be relieved every six or nine months; but it now became so difficult to do this promptly that, men recruited during 1916 either had to wait for release, or were kept to reinforce the mass levy of 1917. It is clear, however, that the discharge process was continuous even if delayed.

Smuts showed much greater energy and dynamism than his predecessors. The 1st Division advanced from Longido, hoping to take the enemy in the rear at Moshi. The 2nd Division attacked Salaita on 9th March. Von Lettow retreated without fighting but put up fierce resistance at Reata and Latema, where 3rd KAR suffered casualties losing 81 men, while others were either missing or wounded. Their popular commanding officer, Lieut-Col. Graham, was among the dead. The 1st Division was much too large a force to advance fast through the difficult country, and it failed to cut off the German retreat. The first phase of the campaign ended with the occupation of Kahe on the Tanga-Moshi railway on 21st March 1916. The Kilimanjaro area was now taken, but Smuts had not destroyed von Lettow and his troops, nor had he ended the campaign. For political reasons, Smuts was unwilling to risk heavy casualties in battle as the truth of Meinertzhagen's comment bears out: "Every man killed in battle means ten invalided with disease".[12] von Lettow had been outmanoeuvred but his casualties were light. Hence, he was not seriously weakened.

In April 1916, it was at last decided to expand the KAR. Therefore, the 2nd and 6th regiments were revived: the former were Nyasa, the later ex-German askari. There were now six regiments with two battalions each. Then the 7th KAR was formed out of the Zanzibar Rifles and Mafia Constabulary, with one battalion. There were finally twenty-two battalions which took over the entire campaign at the end of 1917. The KAR competed with the Carrier Corps for recruits. Smuts suggested picking 3,000 men for the first three new battalions from the 30,000 carriers available in April 1916. The Administrator of North-Eastern Rhodesia was, however, reluctant to deplete his carrier forces by allowing Bemba to be recruited for the new 2nd KAR. The performance of the expanded KAR further demonstrated the superiority of the African soldier and enhanced the status of the carrier. To be fair to the White and Indian troops, it was not their fault that they had been unable to win this terrible war in which the climate was a greater enemy than the Germans.

No longer under the Colonial Office, the KAR were at last imperial troops but theirs is a dismal story of lost opportunities. The KAR should have been expanded in August 1914 and trained by officers with East African experience, too many of whom were wasted on the Western Front. This particularly applied to Colonel Hoskins, Inspector-General KAR. Failure of making him Commander-in-Chief at once was described as "one of the greatest blunders of the war" by a senior officer on the East African Force when writing to the Official Historian.

The second phase of the campaign involved two sweeping movements, to the west and east of the vast plains to the south of Kilimanjaro, meeting along the line of the Central Railway from Dar es Salaam to Lake Tanganyika. After the fall of Kahe, Major-General van Deventer led the 2nd Division along the western route to Dodoma, leaving Arusha on 1st April. The rains had now set in with quite exceptional force whose paralysing effect had not been foreseen. The road crossed wet black cotton soil poached to a morass. Men could only do two miles an hour while a telegraph lorry was only able to move

A K.A.R. Column crossing a river, 1917
   Courtesy of Dr. Clive Irvine

using its winch. Animals and lorries then seem to have provided transport and not the carriers.

It was therefore no small feat by the 2nd Division to have taken Kondoa Irangi half way to the Central Railway, and to have held it on 9th May against a counter-attack led by von Lettow himself. He was able to join his troops there because Smuts' advance from Kahe had not yet begun. The Germans were defeated with severe losses, but when van Deventer reached the Central Railway on 29th July, his division was in very bad shape. It had lost 1,639 horses out of 3,894, and the men were half starved. Brigadier-General Fendall, the administrative chief, had protested against this advance. He pointed out that the division would be cut off on the far side of a piece of country a hundred miles wide, over which supply was bound to be impossible for several months. The division now advanced eastwards along the railway, and on 22nd August, van Deventer at Kilosa reported the extreme exhaustion of his animals and men.

After the fall of Kahe on 21st March, the eastern advance was badly delayed by the rains until 22th May. Smuts with the 1st Division occupied Usambara and Korogwe and followed the railway to Mombo. Had the military and naval commanders got their act together at this point, they could easily have occupied the port of Tanga. This would have simplified supply problems during the southward advance and reduced the suffering of the troops and followers involved. In 1915, a pointless naval bombardment had caused much damage at Tanga, which was finally taken on 3rd July. The ensuring advance down the coast in July and August led to the occupation of Pangani, Bagamoyo and Dar es Salaam. The navy had also bombarded Dar es

Salaam, adding severe damage to the demolition already carried out by the Germans. This greatly impeded efforts to get the port working as the main base for the force. Nevertheless, seaborne forces took Mikindani, Kilwa and Lindi south of the Rufiji.

Naval power was never effectively used in support of the army in this campaign. There seems to have been very little liaison or consultation between the two units as shown by the failure of the navy to prevent arms from reaching the German land forces as had happened before with *Rubens* and *Konigsberg* respectfully. This happened once again in March 1916, when a blockade runner called the *Marie* von *Stettin* slipped past two patrol ships into Sudi bay near Lindi. The Germans salvaged most of her cargo which consisted four 105mm howitzers, two 75mm mountain guns, some machine guns, ammunition and other stores including some well-deserved iron crosses, and a detachment of trained gunners. To von Lettow, this probably meant the difference between being able to carry on or not, as was the case with the *Rubens*. General headquarters heard nothing about it for a month. The acid comment of the Official Military Historian is that, "the affair is not referred to in *Naval Operations*."

The light howitzers were especially welcome to von Lettow. Fighting often took place in a bush which was too dense for gunfire to be observed. Therefore, howitzers and mortars, which lob their shells, were very much more suitable than mountain guns which have high muzzle velocity and flat trajectory. A major improvement to British firepower came with the Stokes mortars which had the extra advantage of being portable by carriers.

The Germans fought a series of stubborn rearguard actions in the face of Smuts' advance through Handeni to Morogoro, which was taken on 26th August. Casualties in battle were heavy; but losses from disease, exhaustion and privation were worse. Most of the mules, oxen and horses died while carriers suffered severely, especially from the demands imposed by the very long marches. The losses of transport animals, both on Smuts' march and on that of van Deventer, was hard to replace, thus throwing an added burden on the carriers during the next phase.

African reminiscences of the horrors of these operations were much more scaring than they were later, when casualty numbers were much higher, as shown by accounts of a number of survivors. For example, after his adventures on the Namanga road, Marius Karatu went as far as Moshi, but then deserted in horror at the bloodshed he had seen, especially a European's body in two halves on each side of a stream. He said that the Germans had sawn it in half, but it was possibly a gruesome result of shellfire as Europeans were certainly afraid of being taken alive by German askari.

Other survivors who recalled the horrors were: Jonathan Okwirri, later a well known senior chief in Nyanza. He was a superior headman of carriers in the Moshi advance. He spent the rest of the war at Tanga and at the Mombasa Carrier Depot. Another was Muthanya wa Muiri, a Meru askari, who served in the Moshi area and later in the Kilwa-Lindi hinterland. He seems to have taken part in one of the attacks on Salaita. The war work of so many of his age group is shown by its name *Kaaria*. Then there was Nguka Nyaoke, who was from South Nyanza. He was first a carrier and later a stretcher bearer with the KAR. He spoke of a long, hard march, apparently ending at Dar es Salaam. Under these circumstances, he could not have trained at Kwa Maleve, the depot for gun carriers, stretcher bearers and other front-line porters at Ngong. Finally, there was William Kwinga Nthenge, who lived near Kiu but began his career at Ngong. He recalled, "From there, I went to Voi and Mwatate . . . we fought our way to Mbuyuni and from there to Dar es Salaam, whence we were shipped to Mombasa until the war ended".[13]

Francis Brett Young, whose book *Marching on Tanga* is well known, was probably the most gifted and sensitive writer with the force. As a medical officer, he had Nyanza stretcher bearers and orderlies working under him and their cheerfulness and courage deeply impressed him. Another important European witness was Frank Weston, Bishop of Zanzibar, who led his own Carrier Corps on the Handeni Road and into Dar es Salaam.

The Germans did extensive damage to the Usambara and Central Railway, both of which the British had by now controlled. However, they had "failed to take the one step we feared of pulling up track and throwing miles of fastenings into the bush", says the railway historian.[14] The Indian Sappers and Miners worked with great speed and skill, restoring 300 miles of track in three months which was surely one of the most remarkable performances by any unit throughout the campaign. The troops were having a very bad time: the 1st Division at Kilwa, the 2nd at Dodoma, and the 3rd around the Uluguru Mountains were all given "an appalling report" by their chief medical officer, which augured badly for Smuts' southward thrust.

Two other invasions of German East Africa took place in 1916, neither of which was under Smuts' control. The first was the

Anglo-Belgian advance on Tabora, the main inland centre of trade and transport. The Belgians had taken over Congo from King Leopold in 1907. Their administration was rudimentary. Their colonial troops numbered about 9,000 but they lacked enough carriers on whom they were heavily dependent in Uganda; first 120,000 "job" porters and then 8,429 men known as the Belgian Congo Carrier Corps or "Carbels". Under General Tombeur, their first move was to occupy Ruanda-Urundi.

Having taken Ujiji, the main port on Lake Tanganyika, the Belgians pushed east along the Central Railway. Meanwhile, the British took Bukoba (which they had raided in 1915, destroying the wireless station), and then Mwanza, both on Lake Victoria. The first troops into Mwanza were Major J. J. Drought's scantily dressed Skin Corps "to the intense annoyance" of Sir Charles Crewe, the British commander, a South African politician turned general. Crewe's relations with Tombeur, his Belgian colleague, was so bad that they seldom communicated. He suffered further disappointment of reaching Tabora six days later than the Belgians on 25th September 1916.

In an undated paper, the British Military Liaison Officer with the Belgians, Major Ewart Grogan, wrote that Belgians had no reliable formulae for calculating porter requirements; they had no experience of porter organisation, and no Europeans capable of it. "Porters are merely dumped in bulk onto a combatant unit and have to take their chance", wrote Grogan. Owing to the terrible wastage among their porters, their forces could easily become immobile at a moment's notice. There were also enough soldiers' women to increase the food required by 20%, but it was the price which had to be paid for the morale of their force under the prevailing circumstances. Many had been away from home for three years and were on the verge of mutiny. They had about 10,000 porters but needed 18,000 and half were German East Africa men; another 3,000 were from Katanga, and had established some organic relationship with the troops to whom they were attached.

The Nyasaland Field Force under Brigadier-General Northey, 2,000 strong, began their advances in May 1916, taking Neu Langenburg (later called Tukuyu) on 29th May. They then pushed on to occupy Iringa, the capital of the southern highlands, on 29th August. Their line of communication was by now nearly 200 miles long and depended on carriers who were recruited throughout the Nyasaland Protectorate. Carrier service lacked the glamour of the KAR. They called it *thangata* or the war of *thangata*, a word meaning "work without profit". It was used to describe the forced labour of the colonial regime. The carriers' lot involved grievous drudgery and hunger in a cause which meant nothing to them. Here too they were the backbone of the Europeans war and not for nothing did Northey declare: "I would award the palm of merit to the tenga-tenga" (as carriers were called in Nyasaland).

After the British had crossed Central Railway, Watkins wrote:

> "The lines of communication back to the Tanga-Moshi railway were now of unprecedented length, and the first step was to convert the Central Railway... into the base line of the force... as rapidly as possible, the situation being much ameliorated, if not saved from absolute disaster, by the fitting of trolley wheels to transport vehicles of various kinds.... The first however only got to Dodoma on October 6th.... The interval was one of short rations and considerable

sufferings... *and where the troops suffer the condition of the followers is apt to be pitiable"* (Author's italics).[15]

That then was the Smuts offensive.

The drive to Rufiji

We were working - cutting bush and carrying bullets, taking them to the river called Rufiji (Kinyanjui wa Mukura, carrier)

General Smuts had allowed his duel with von Lettow to become something of an obsession. His impatience with supply problems drove him and his exhausted army on. He argued, "Hunger! Thirst! There are no such things when the success of a great operation hangs in the balance."[16] This extraordinary statement deserves repetition because Smuts was losing touch with military reality. No operation can succeed if the men are dying of thirst or exhaustion. Having made Dar es Salaam his base, Smuts could have rested his army on the Central Railway as the troops, especially the South Africans, were fever-stricken and exhausted, and the hospitals were full.

Colonel von Lettow refused to fight at Morogoro, as Smuts had hoped. "To me, this idea was never intelligible", wrote von Lettow. "Being so very much the weaker party, it was surely madness to await at this place the junction of the hostile columns."[17] So the third phase of Smuts' campaign began. As von Lettow had expected, Smuts again made flanking movements, this time on each side of the Uluguru Mountains. Pushing straight on from Morogoro, his two columns fought their way south until they met at Kisaki on 15th September in appalling weather, the rains having been two months early.

Smuts was once again very unlucky with the weather. A South African officer, Deneys Reitz, described conditions in the Kisaki area as follows:

> "Day and night the mosquitoes buzzed . . . malaria and dysentery were rife. The forest swarmed with tsetse fly, and our horses began to die at such a rate that, weakened as we were, we could not muster enough hands to bury the rotting carcasses .... With the heavy rain, the carriers failed, and where we had been on short commons before, we went on shorter now. A road had been opened from Morogoro east of the Uluguru Mountains, for the transporting of supplies, but the Tulo River and other streams were up, and all the country was inches deep in black mud."[16]

It became worse later.

"Already, as one of the main lessons of the campaign, it was indisputable that in tropical Africa, troops other than native Africans had proved in general unsuited", wrote the Official Historian. Except for the 25th Royal Fusiliers, the white troops departed: 12,000 South Africans, the Rhodesians, and the North Lancs. In September, Smuts began a final drive with a flanking move based on the newly captured port of Kilwa Kisiwani. In October and November, Hoskins advanced with a division of fresh Indian troops and new KAR units. West African troops were now in action with the Nigerian Brigade taking part in the crossing of the Rufiji River in heavy rain on new year's day in 1917. Unfortunately, ten men drowned.

Then the Germans withdrew to the south bank as floods rose."[19]

The advance on the Rufiji was the final horror of 1916, and the problems of supply the most severe. Writes Watkins in his Report:

> "The practice of relieving carriers every six or nine months which had obtained throughout 1915, had proved impossible during the advance. By September 1916, when they were suddenly called upon for a supreme effort on short rations, the men were already debilitated and overworked. As a final torture, the rains broke early and converted large areas into swamp, throwing still more work on the Carrier, who ... on the Dodoma-Iringa road had to carry on nine miles mostly waist-deep in water, much of it on raised duck walks made of undressed poles laid side by side .... The sufferings and casualties of this period from September 1916 to March 1917 will never be fully known."[20]

Heavy casualties among porters and donkeys on the Dodoma-Iringa line were mentioned by Captain Downes on the Nigeria Regiment, while discussing transport and supply problems. He concluded that there possibly couldn't be any other theatre of war possessing so difficult a line of communication as the road from Mikesse (near Morogoro) to the Rufiji, which was now the main artery of the advance. Heavy lorries theoretically carrying 60,000 lbs daily for the first forty-one miles to Summit reduced the road to mud. Ford box-cars, called "jiggers" because they could go almost anywhere , did the next 35 miles to Duthumi. Mules and animal transport carts did a further 45 miles to Kimbambawe.

In practice, carriers, who were supposed to carry only on the last lap to the Rufiji seem to have been used on all sections. The first two were precarious for lorries even before the rains, and only 5,000 lbs daily had been coming through during the two weeks after Christmas 1916. The officer in command on the Rufiji increasingly sent curt letters to Dar es Salaam about the meagre rations reaching his men, but he later found the road sufficiently formidable even after the rains. He apologised personally at every office in general headquarters . Now that he had seen the road, his only wonder was that anything at all had been got up. Of the Duthumi-Tulo section, Downes says:

> "The distance is not more than 12 miles, but for nearly the whole way the road led through the worst sort of stinking black mud. [The water was knee-deep and sometimes above the waist.] To make matters worse, large numbers of cattle and donkeys had died in the swamp, and having rotted, the stench was too hard for words ."[21]

During the rains, motor transport from Summit to Tulo did only sixteen miles a day, and the Mua river was crossed by a trolley on an overhead wire, which took five hours. There was another overhead trolley at the Ngeta river, beyond which the water was frequently waist deep for two miles. Crocodiles sometimes haunted the path and killed carriers. The putrefying bodies of carriers, mules and donkeys littered the road. The 3,000 troops on the Rufiji were fed by an army of 12,000 carriers. Overworked transport drivers fell sick in such numbers that few lasted more than a month.

The plight of the carrier with his load of over 50 pounds passes imagination. Cold, wet, sick with dysentery and pneumonia, his only food being half-cooked porridge made of maize meal which was probably fermenting from being soaked in its sack, many a man staggered off the road to die in the reeking mud. These rains therefore reduced fighting man and follower to a common level of misery.

Smuts' refusal to halt on the Central Railway was alone enough to destroy the offensive strength of his army. He missed his last chance of sparing his men worse sufferings by pushing on to the Rufiji, instead of withdrawing from Kisaki in September when the weather broke. But von Lettow shows his usual insight in the following comment: "General Smuts realized that his blow had failed. He sent me a letter calling upon me to surrender, by which he showed that, as far as force was concerned, he had reached the end of his resources."[22] Many British officers agreed with Lettow.

By the new year, the Quartermaster-General's Department had left Smuts in no doubt as to the gravity of the transport crisis. A memorandum of 6th December told of the shortage of carriers: "The D.M.L. [Watkins] is doing his best, but as far as I can see (unless we get Belgian help) we will have to rely on local carriers, and the most we can hope for is 5,000."[23]

The bid for Belgian help had failed at a high level, as a telegram from the War Office made clear that the protracted negotiations with Belgians was due entirely to the attitude adopted by them; that negotiations for their further military cooperation would be dropped indefinitely. Another memorandum of 9th January ended: "I honestly cannot see how we are going to feed the troops in view of the serious mechanical transport situation."[24] On 31st December 1916, there were only 62,334 effective carriers left out of about 150,000 recruited from the East Africa Protectorate and German East Africa.

Despite all this, on his return to South Africa, Smuts addressed a public rally in Pretoria, saying that German resistance was broken. In March, he said that the campaign in East Africa might be said to be over although von Lettow was trying to keep going. He assured the public that it was merely the remnant of an army that was left, and not a formidable fighting force. He continued to say that the white troops had been unequal to the climate, but the new native infantry were magnificent; that in May, they could move, and the thing would be finished. Smuts' claim to have trained the new KAR battalions was much resented by British officers who pointed out that the initiative had come from Hoskins. Smuts went on to London where he joined the Imperial War Cabinet in June 1917. The belief that he had defeated von Lettow still lingers; but Smuts was a politician rather than a soldier, a master of propaganda. In Afrikaans, he was Slim Janie, meaning "Crafty Johnnie". Maybe, the South African public were less impressed than the British; battle casualties may have been light, but about 60% of the South Africans sent to German East Africa were invalided at home, sick.

The Remnant of an army: 1917

I was present when Risasi Camp wa shelled. I escaped injury though many died. Once, I was shot at and unfortunately lost my finger from a bullet wound (Lazaro Maende, ammunitions carrier)

On 20th January 1917, General Smuts handed over to General Hoskins the task of finishing off Colonel von Lettow and what

Smuts called his "remnant of an army". The same day, the rains intensified, thereby making the supply position of Smuts' troops, already desperate, much worse. Plans were being drawn up for the new campaign which was expected to be much more than a mere "mopping-up operation". Hoskins presented the War Office with demands for more men and materials on a scale which showed that Smuts' sanguine statements were nothing but wishful thinking. They gravely embarrassed the war cabinet. In the words of Brigadier-General Fendall, Hoskins "had taken over from Smuts an instrument blunted and useless for any offensive action".[25] Hoskins used the four months that he was in command, during which the weather ruled out active operations, to make his army fit to take the field again.

Hoskins' first aim was to make the Rufiji the northern baseline, though the notorious road from Mikesse via Summit and Duthumi had to be kept up. There were now about 7,000 German troops, half of whom were in the southern and eastern side of the Rufiji; a quarter in the mountains between Tukuyu and Songea, and the rest divided between the Mahenge plateau and the Lindi hinterland. They would either hold the whole area or concentrate on a rich area like Songea, but Hoskins knew that whichever course the enemy took, his eventual retirement into Portuguese East Africa was possible.

There would be four columns: First, a brigade under Colonel Taylor was to advance on Mahenge from Iringa. Secondly, the Nigerian Brigade was to meet it in the same area, based on the Rufiji. Thirdly, the two Kilwa brigades under Brigadier-General Hennyngton were to strike inland towards Liwale using the sixty miles of tramway built mainly by Taita labour from Voi District. Finally, there was the Lindi force under Brigadier-General O'Grady. The backbone of the force was now African;

the Gold Coast Regiment having been part of "Hanforce". All would depend on motor transport and porters.

Hoskins protested at the withdrawal of troops, guns and aircraft to Egypt and was also short of railway material and personnel. He asked for 500 Reo American light lorries, and the War Office, taken aback by all these demands for a campaign which was supposed to be over, promised 200 for mid-May. If Hoskins' minimum requirement of 400 lorries and 800 drivers was not met by the end of April, he would need another 12,000 porters, thirty of whom would do the work of one lorry. There may have been 40,000 carriers in hand but 160,000 would be wanted. The Nigerian and Gold Coast troops were accompanied by 8,992 West African carriers. Although more were needed from Portuguese East Africa, this involved questions of diplomacy not easily to be resolved, at least not until von Lettow did so by invading Portuguese East Africa. Hoskins asked for 15,000 extra carriers a month, to replace the "wastage" which was expected to be 15%. This meant nearly three times the number available in December 1916, when recruitment had been hard enough.

The occupied German territory north of the Central Railway was now under a civil administrator, Mr. Horace Byatt. His first duty was to supply military labour. The south of the Railway was controlled by the military, who were much less concerned with political repercussions than were Byatt, or the governments of the East Africa Protectorate and Uganda. General Staff's plans were now to exact from the civil governments their supreme effort in labour recruiting. This meant the "mass Levy".

Watkins' explanation as to why so many carriers were needed

then was that the new campaign would be in a country without modern communications and with little white settlement. The enemy could leave few supplies or able-bodied men and could wage a guerrilla war, having no fixed centre, with the aim surrounding him. This would require 160,000 carriers with 16,000 replacements a month. The East Africa Protectorate was to produce 67,779 and Uganda 10,947 up to 31 July 1917, when there would be about 120,000 on Military Labour Bureau books, besides personal servants and casual labour. Owing to the difficulties of shipping such large numbers, this number was the nearest approach ever made to estimated requirements.

In the British territories, Nyanza Province excelled as a source of labour, because it was the most closely administered. However, its population was not much larger than that of some other areas. Since 1907, the P.C. had been John Ainsworth whose work in carrier recruiting had already been praised by the Quartermaster-General, Gen. Ewart as follows:

> "Watkins and I were saying only yesterday that if it had not been for you and your efforts we should have been in a really bad way.... The porters you have sent are simply invaluable, and it is solely to your having had them in the last 3 weeks that the force below the Rufiji [sic] has been able to move at all... it was disappointing that the push on 1st January didn't succeed but *the country is so impossible that they invariably break any net the General may spread for them.*" [Author's italics][26]

Perhaps staff officers already had little faith in plans to encircle the enemy in thick bush country, when Smuts had failed to do so in the relatively open Kilimanjaro area.

At the end of February 1917, Hoskins formally asked the Governor of the East Africa Protectorate for Ainsworth's services as Military Commissioner for Labour, with the rank of full colonel, to run the mass levy which was now necessary since he was plainly the only man suitable for such a position . The labour in the reserves was said to be nearly exhausted, and Provincial Commissioners in the White Highland areas namely, the Rift Valley, Laikipia and Uasin Gishu, had already been asked to recruit.

Ainsworth soon announced his plans: it was reckoned that there were 195,000 suitable men in Nyanza, Kenia, Ukamba and Seyidie. A capital draft of 30,000 was to be raised by the end of April, with reinforcing drafts of 13,000 a month in June and July. Since motor and animal transport had become virtually impossible in the theatre of operations, *it virtually became a porters' war* as in fact it had always been . Men who had already served could be recalled if they had been home for three months. It was hoped that this massive effort would finish the campaign in a few months. It is impossible however to say how often a man served twice as a carrier, but plural enlistment was probably uncommon in practice, because so many men were unfit from the effects of previous service.

Recruitment went remarkably smoothly in the districts of the East Africa Protectorate and Uganda, for which Ainsworth was also responsible. Nevertheless, there was a controversy with the acting governor of Uganda which we will see in the next section. The levy was suddenly called off in August 1917, though the war was far from over. Ainsworth was absolutely certain that the East Africa Protectorate officials had done their best to put up all available men; and that they had undoubtedly come to the end of their resources. Officials were worried about possible unrest, both in the East Africa Protectorate and in the occupied enemy areas. There were no more men, and the attempt to defeat von Lettow by the mass levy had failed, like other expeditions.

When the Rufiji became the base line, casual labour was increasingly used behind it by contracts with local chiefs. On the Mikesse line, the local native at last undertook the whole burden of communication, supplying his own requirements besides a surplus of food for transport to other areas. Carriers from the East Africa Protectorate highlands, like the Kikuyu Mission Volunteers, worked on the Dodoma to Iringa line, where the climate suited them. They supported the Belgian advance from Kilosa to Mahenge which fell on 9th October 1917.

> "The porters' war" was actually directed by General van Deventer, who took over from General Hoskins on 29th May. This had been decided over a month earlier by the Imperial War Cabinet. Smuts had said that he thought Hoskins had lost grip of the operations and perhaps had become tired. It was agreed that van Deventer should be asked to succeed Hoskins. Opinion among British officers, who greatly resented the change of command, was that Hoskins was sacrificed on the alter of political expediency. Once again the services of this experienced officer were wasted."[27]

Hoskins' fate had already been decided when, in a wire to the War Office on 4th May, he commented on a report by Smuts in *The Times*, and said that the report might have been conveying a wrong impression as to the probability of the campaign being brought to a speedy conclusion; and the enemy's force being well controlled, "If contrary to above is believed, misunderstanding and disappointment will arise," he advised.[28] The actual situation, Hoskins explained, was that the war would last even longer if von Lettow dispersed over a wide area or crossed the Ruvuma. Smuts must surely have been well aware that what Hoskins said was true.

These warnings were borne out by the fierce resistance of the Germans to the attempts by van Deventer's four columns to trap them, culminating in the fearsome battle of Mahiwa, from 16th to 19th October. The British casualties were about 2,500 men, over half of the force engaged. The Lindi column in particular was so shattered that they were out of action until after the Germans had escaped southward. The German casualties of 500 out of 1,500 was proportionately even more severe, as von Lettow could not make good such losses though he could claim a tactical victory. This bitter and bloody fighting gave the lie to Smuts' political showmanship. One wonders whether he or van Deventer would have involved a large number of South African troops in a battle like Mahiwa.

The Long March : 1917-1918

Keya dibuoro nindo gichuma oko! oko! (In the KAR, a soldier sleeps out with his weapons, and dies, dies far from home)
Luo song- Odandayo Agweli, 4th KAR)

The long march of Colonel Paul von Lettow-Vorbeck and his men after the battle of Mahiwa was the last phase of the East African campaign. The Germans' military skill and toughness under this leader of genius had kept them going for over three years. Von Lettow was a brilliant administrator and improviser. He was the first to recognise the large windfalls of armaments provided, unwittingly, by British military and naval incompetence in Tanga; also the *Konigsberg guns* and the two blockade runners described earlier. Added to Lettows' ingenuity were two vital assets; a well organised colonial administration and a strong economy. Governor von Schnee therefore deserves more credit than he is usually allowed. Evidently, extraordinary ingenuity was used to produce cloth, rope, soap, rubber, petrol, spirits, quinine substitute, boots: the list is endless. It is a good illustration of how determined people can successfully resist economic and military sanctions.

Nevertheless, Mahiwa was decisive because it weakened the *Schutztruppe* so much that they could no longer risk a major engagement or maintain themselves in German East Africa. This was emphasised by the surrender near Kilimanjaro on 2nd October of a maverick German column of about 1,500 askari and carriers who had been fighting their way north since February. The leaders were acting against von Lettow's orders, but unknown to them, about 4,000 British and Belgian troops had been engaged in hunting them down; large numbers of carriers were also involved as they were needed for the mass levy. The effect of the raid was that it dislocated the British logistical and administrative services, including carrier recruiting, in an area which was supposed to be far behind the battle line.

The offensive

The British occupied all the productive areas of German East Africa after the Mahiwa battle. Von lettow had no alternative but to invade Portuguese East Africa with a small and highly mobile column, having abandoned about 50 Europeans and 600 Africans who could no longer march. Accordingly, the Germans crossed the Ruvuma River into Portuguese territory on 25th November 1917, with 1,700 askari and 5,000 followers. Despite his differences with von Lettow, Governor von Schnee was not left behind. The Germans soon routed a Portuguese force, capturing enough arms, ammunition, food and medical supplies to enable them fight on, and to replace most of the remaining 1871 rifles. Using captured askaris as carriers, they marched on and re-crossed the Ruvuma on 28th September 1918, after successfully fighting off British columns which had tried to intercept them.

The British had established bases on the coast at Port Amelia, Lumbo and Quelimane, where carrier depots were opened. They then advanced inland in order to stop the Germans who easily evaded their columns, and successfully attacked the weakly defended British posts. Nevertheless, the long march ended in North-East Rhodesia at Kasama, which the Germans took on 12th November 1918, the day after the Armistice in Europe. Paul von Lettow-Vorbeck retained the initiative to the end; won the last engagement of the first world war, and can fairly be called the most successful German commander. He had completely succeeded in his war aims, which cost the British dearly in human and material resources. The resulting suffering of the East African people cannot be exaggerated. Lord Kitchener and others were fully vindicated in thinking that it would have been enough to conquer the Kilimanjaro area and the ports, which could have been done with smaller forces of African troops.

The 1917 offensive was successful in that it eliminated or expelled all remaining German forces in German East Africa. The East African Force, the Belgians and the Nyasaland Field Force under General Northey (Norforce) were now all linked up at Iringa in the southern highlands. In August, the Military Labour Bureau took responsibility for Norforce carriers, who originally came from Nyasaland.

A recruiting depot was opened at Tukuyu (Neu Langenburg), but communication was so difficult that little use could be made of Norforce carriers. Meanwhile, Porter recruiting and political liaison with the Portuguese was managed by Military Labour Burea officers like Major F.M.S. Stokes. Fighting columns often moved too fast to keep in touch with lines of communication. Stokes therefore had to organise his own link section and recruiting organisation because he thought that senior British political officers were too inclined to meet Portuguese wishes. This could be highly detrimental to recruiting, especially when Portuguese askaris used to collect taxes, seizing women in default. Therefore, men naturally refused to leave their families unprotected.

During 1917, the British had been supplying carriers to the Belgians; mostly mass levy porters like the Kikuyu Mission Volunteers. A final change in organisation was the replacement of the gang system by the individual system for registering and paying carriers. This was because most followers now worked at posts on long lines of communication, or at bases and depots, and so moved about much less. Under the individual system, each follower was identified by his number and file at the Nairobi Carrier Depot if he came from the East Africa, or at Dar es Salaam if he was from German East Africa. The significance of this extended beyond mere bureaucracy because it protected

A Column of Carriers on the March in German East Africa
Courtesy of Dr. Clive Irvine

the rights of the men and enhanced their status. The Military Labour Bureau became the Military Labour Corps in March 1918, when most of its members had ceased to be involved in

The Watkins Report explains that the part played by labour began to assume a character it subsequently retained during this period. Bases with wharves, warehouses and water supplies, were established. The Kilwa Railway and many roads were built as the troops advanced. Motor transport took over from carriers, but where swamps or rain ruled out motorised forms of transport the carrier took its place, while his brother the labourer, fought the deprivations of the rain on the causeways and bridges of the roads.

Reminiscences

It was a campaign of long marches, particularly for the Germans, their askaris and their carriers, but hardly less for their enemies, the British, with their great army of African followers. The contrast with the static warfare on the Western Front could hardly be more stark. Any man, however, who is taken away from his home against his will and sent to war, is spiritually on a long march or undergoing a "wilderness experience", to use the term coined by John Arthur, leader of the Kikuyu Mission Volunteers. The men who spent longest time away from their homes were, on the whole, those from German East Africa and the East Africa Protectorate. For example, Kimumo Kitui's personal march began from his home near Kiu. After a week at Kariakor, the Nairobi Carrier Depot, he went as a stretcher bearer to Tsavo and from there marched via Taveta and Moshi to Dodoma, and on by land to Mahiwa where Dr. Ralph Scott, later Director of Medical Services in Tanganyika, also served.

In the Battlefields

Kimumo's story is corroborated by Dr. Scott who told the author about the bravery of his Kamba stretcher bearers. Said Kimumo with evident pride:

> "I got a gun at Kilwa. I became a soldier, KAR Company D of Captain Ngomoli. After Mahiwa, there were many vacancies in the KAR ranks. I was under fire many times, and got a bullet wound in the leg. I went on to Port Amelia and Nyasaland, and returned by sea to Mombasa."[29]

Odandayo Mukhenye Agweli was the askari whose Luo victory song is quoted at the beginning of this section. His home was in Bunyala, west of Central Nyanza. He had visited Morogoro, Iringa and Mahenge. He recounted,

> "At Lindi, we had some battles. Indian troops joined us here to fight the enemy. The actual area was called Kampi ya Ndege (Aeroplane Camp)... using mortars we levelled the whole place before attacking ... to this day, I still do not know why we fought the Germans and how the war began. Though we admired the European ways of fighting, we were still left wondering why so many people had to die. In our tribal wars, the number of the dead was never very big."[30]

Agweli and his neighbour Asembo Odera, were in the 4th (Uganda) KAR. Odera's number was 1097. He lost a leg. He greatly admired German courage and strength in battle. According to him, they used to fight from the tops of trees like monkeys. He said that so many people were fighting on the British side that they sometimes shot at each other by mistake. He also claimed to have distinguished between German and

British gunfire:

> "I once encountered a German soldier [It is unclear whether black or white]. He did not shoot at me, but just warned me that if I moved that would be my end. *'Wewe bwana, leo ni leo. Utakufa tu. Songa karibu, utaona,'* said the German soldier."[31]

According to both Agweli and Odera, the famine which followed the end of the war was called *Keya* in Bunyala after the KAR.

Front-line porters, carrying ammunition, machine-guns, parts of mountain guns, mortars or their bombs performed duties as dangerous as those of the fighting men. They could not take cover as quickly as soldiers, if suddenly under fire because of the loads they were carrying. Lazaro Maende, quoted at the beginning of section 3.5, lost a finger. Ngugi, a Kiambu machine-gun carrier, was shot in the arm when carrying a load.

Anglo-German relations seemed ambiguous to the carriers as can be gathered from M'Inoti wa Tirikamu, a Meru carrier who had worked on the Namanga road who said:

> "We naturally wondered why white men hated each other so much. They looked so much like brothers. We asked ourselves: 'Do they fight for land, or for the power to rule, or is it because they are all white, or why?"[32]

On the other hand, when not fighting with each other, the British and the Germans were reported to have seemed very friendly: "German officers would come to the British camp, and we would see them talking, not as enemies would do. This often surprised and confused us,"[33] said Muasya Maitha and Umoa Mbatha of Muthetheni, Machakos District(Umoa was a carrier headman, and Muasya an ammunition carrier). Truces were however, not unusual in African wars. It was at any rate now clear to the Africans that the British were not the only European tribe. Probably many realised, like M'Inoti and the Kikuyu Mission Volunteers at Kahuhia, that the whites fought for power and land.

All Europeans recognised after the war that the entire campaign had depended on the Africans. As soldiers, they could stand the rigours of warfare in a tropical country much better than the Europeans and Indians. Wrote Richard Meinertzhagen:

> "The King's African Rifles have shown up well. They are well officered and have never once failed us. Their pluck, endurance and discipline have stood the test of war and on all sides one hears nothing but admiration for them".[34]

The new battalions were inadequately trained, and the new officers were, not surprisingly, sub-standard. Of the carriers however, Meinertzhagen had nothing but praise:

> "With scant discipline they have proved themselves on more than one occasion to be stout-hearted fellows and cheerful in adversity. On three occasions they have stood their ground when South African and Indian troops have moved back. And what some of these gallant porters have suffered will never be known".[35]

Rudyard Kipling's aphorism that *the carriers were the feet and hands of the army* summarises their contribution to the success of the Campaign more accurately than any other words can do.

Unfortunately, the long march ended half way for very many of the carriers — *oko! oko!* as the Luo song has it; in death — very, very far from home.

Notes

1. Kenya National Archives, DC/TTA/3/2. Reminiscences of S.H. La Fontaine. ADC Taveta in 1914, whose agents correctly forecast the German attack on Taveta.
2. Shepperson and Price, *Independent African*. 234-235.
3. Meinertzhagen, *Army Diary*, 106-109, 112. 116-117.
4. Edwin P. Hoyt, Jr., *The Germans Who Never Lost* (London: Leslie Frewin. 1968), *passim*..
5. Savage and Munro, JAH, 7, 2(1966), 314, n.6.
6. Watkins Papers, Staff Correspondence and Confidential file.
7. Public Record Office, Cabinet Office Papers 45/31, Wapshare to War Office. 10 March 1915; Horden, *Operations in EA*, 139-141.
8. Watkins Papers, staff correspondence and confidential file.
9. Ibid.
10. Ibid.
11. Public Records Office, Cabinet Office papers 45/31, note by Lieutenant-Colonel L.M. Davies on Salaita, 17 Oct. 1934; *Army Diary*, 165.
12. *Army Diary*, 166, 176-200.
13. Interview 13 Dec. 1969.
14. Hill, *Permanent Way*, Vol. II, 167-169; see Public Records Office. Cabinet Office Papers 45/16, Major-General R.E.. Ewart and Subordinates, on unnecessary supplies blocking trolley line, clearing Dar harbour.
15. Watkins Report, para. 27; author's italics.
16. Hancock, *Smuts*, 421; Armstrong, *Smuts*, 216.
17. von Lettow, *Reminiscences*, 149.
18. D. Reitz, *Trekking on* (London: Faber, 1933), 145.
19. Hordern. *Operations in EA*, 393, Public Record Office, Cabit Office Papers 45/31C, Lieutenant-Colonel Crofton, and Cabinet Office papers 45/30. Major Bremmer.
20. Watkins Report, paragraph 28.
21. Downes, *Nigerians*, 109-114; see also Public Records Office, Cabinet Office Papers 44/6, 92-94: four of the five stages were supposed to be by motor: Dobbs to the General Officer Commanding-in-chief, 9 Jan. 1917, only 5,000 a day reaching Rufiji, when 50,000 were needed; later, it was worked by casual labou,r 12,002 were recruited at "Summit": Watkins Report, App. I, Table II.
22. von Lettow-Vorbeck, *My Reminiscences of East Africa* (London: Hurst and Blackett, 1920).
23. Public Records Office (PRO), Cabinet Office Papers (CAB) 44/6, memo by Adjutant and Quartermaster General, 6 Dec. 1916.

24 PRO, CAB 44/6. Dobbs to Smuts. 9 Jan. 1917.
25 PRO, CAB 44/9. 45/31c; Fendall, EAF. 99-101/
26 Ainsworth Papers. Rhodes House Mss Afr. 379-382: 381, Ewart to Ainsworth, 31 Jan. 1917.
27 Watkins Papers. Movements and General Staff Plan; PRO, CAB 23/2. p. 129. War Cabinet Minutes. 23 April 1917: van Deventer was *asked* not ordered. to take the command. showing that it was a political appointment. as Brigadier-General Fendall (EAF. 101).
28 PRO, CAB 44/9. Hoskins to Chief of the Imperial General Staff, 4 May 1917.
29 Notes kindly given by Fred Katule, Machakos.
30 & 31 Notes kindly given by Felix Osodo; Ertiman Gendia and David Sperling kindly helped with the translation.
32 Notes kindly given by Gervase Mutua.
33 Interview at Muthetheni. Machakos. 14 June 1969.
34 Meinertzhagen. *Army Diary.*
35 Ibid. pg 202-3.

Chapter Four

Carrier Units

The Bishop of Zanzibar's Carrier Corps

Truly our Lord Bishop is a great man! . . . when we laid down at night did he not pray with us? And when we arose in the morning, did he not pray with us again?

Missionaries made notable contributions towards the war effort in medicine, hospitals, convalescent camps, intelligence and political work, and in leading Carrier Corps. There are excellent descriptions of two such units by the men who led them. These were Frank Weston's Zanzibar Carrier Corps in 1916 and John Arthur's Kikuyu Mission Volunteers in 1917. Indeed, there seems to be no better accounts of carriers at work than Weston's account on a column march, and Arthur's work on the "dumping" or relay system on an established line of communication.

Early in the war, it was "business as usual" in the East Africa Protectorate and Uganda. But in German East Africa, British missionaries and their followers, that is, the Church Missionary Society (CMS) in the north-west, and the Universities' Mission to Central Africa (UMCA) in the south and east, were cruelly persecuted. Other accounts give witness to this persecution. For instance, Dr. R. V. Dolbey, who had previously been a prisoner of war in Germany, confirms the notorious and degrading treatment suffered at Tabora by British Missionary interns. The *Proceedings* of the CMS also gives accounts of great cruelty to

African Christians. A UMCA convert, S. Sehoza, wrote a book on his experiences titled *A Year in Chains*. There is also a file on "Atrocities in Vanga District" in the Kenya National Archives. Though it is often said that the war did not concern the Africans, a German victory would hardly have been to their advantage.

The German invasion of Belgium had enabled the British to enter the war as a crusade. The ensuing atrocity stories were however much exaggerated. The British, whose own record was not perfect, tended to pass such exaggerated stories on to the Africans but surviving members of the Kikuyu Mission Volunteers at Kahuhia, Murang'a District, were able to make an objective analysis of the war. They said,

> "The Germans and the British were fighting for power, each seeking to have a larger territory than the other. We thought the British would win when they drove the Germans out of Voi and Kisii, and then capture Tanga and Dar es Salaam. The difference between them and the Germans was that the Germans were men of violence, while the British were men of thought."[1]

Frank Weston was Bishop of Zanzibar, one of several Anglican dioceses covering southern German East Africa, Nyasaland and Northern Rhodesia under UMCA, a society founded in 1857 under the direct inspiration of David Livingstone. UMCA represented the High Church or Anglo-Catholic tradition in the Church of England. Weston thought that the CMS missionaries were so eager to compromise with the Church of Scotland and other Protestant societies especially during the ecumenical conference at Kikuyu in 1913, that they were verging on heresy.

He was more forthright and prophetic too in his views on the war and Germany. He believed that the war was caused by the sins of Europe in general and of Germany in particular: He argued,

> "German theology had got rid of Christ .German ethics had rejected his teaching in favour of might .German psychology justified lust, impurity and shameful vice in all this, Germany was only representing Europe. In each nation, you will find some or other of these sins; she has them all, and glories in them."[2]

As the British advanced into German East Africa, they were recruiting porters, both in occupied territory and in Zanzibar. Though Weston's diocese was centred on the island, the greater area was on the mainland. He was therefore, heavily involved in the war and was ready to do his bit. When he and his Roman Catholic colleague protested the recruitment methods reminiscent of the press gang, he was challenged to form his own contingent.

In June 1916, Weston took up the challenge and flung himself with enthusiasm into the task. He had 560 men within a few weeks. He drilled them himself, and with the help of buglers of the Zanzibar Scouts and later by a Goan band, he taught them how to form a line, lift and carry loads and stretchers. The recruits were soon responsive to a word or a whistle. The Bishop had the rank of Major, unpaid and ungazetted at his own request on condition that he could command the force. Subalterns were: two mission laymen, C.M. Baker and A.A. Richardson, a Zanzibar government official, B.C. Johnstone, and Lieutenant-Commander R. N. Clarke. Then there were four mission teachers as clerks and evangelists. They were the Rev. J.B. Mdoe, William Swedi, Henery Kelezi and Alban Ali. The men who had come forward eagerly to join the Bishop were mostly Zanzibaris, with Muslims predominating, but there were Christians also, especially the catechumens. Some pagans volunteered too.

The training period in Zanzibar lasted five weeks and the excellent discipline that prevailed is shown by the fact that they had only three police cases and not one of them was serious. Weston showed his practical sense of the men's welfare in two ways. First, aware of the chaos attending the start of the regular Carrier Corps, he was careful to enlist men under their right names only, which he was probably able to do because of the trust he inspired. Secondly, his Corps would include more literate men than any group of servicemen hitherto. He therefore arranged for a supply of postcards, thus giving us one of our few pieces of evidence in an African hand; that of a Zanzibari porter who wrote:

> "Truly our Lord Bishop is a great man! Did he not call us and gather us all together? Did he not drill us, and go for marches with us every day? Truly he is a great man, for he came over the sea with us, and when we reached the mainland he marched with us, he slept with us, he ate with us, and when we laid down at night, did he not pray with us? And when we arose in the morning, did he not pray with us again?"[3]

In July 1916, they moved to Tanga, which they found to be badly smashed up by the naval bombardment. Here, they doubled their number to over 1,000 and were given four tasks: one, to enclose the town with barbed wire; two, to safeguard the camp; three, to work in the docks; four, to help clean up and police the town. Then, leaving Richardson to meet another 500 recruits from Mombasa, Weston and Baker set out with 1,034 men for Moheza, Korogwe and Handeni. More mission recruits came in enroute and at Korogwe, the Bishop was able to inspect his own mission where a UMCA priest was combining pastoral and political work. Here, he had to hand over 300 men to the Royal Engineers, as his column set off with stores for Ndarema Depot, near Handeni. The journey was perilous as Weston's account shows:

> "Never was there a road like that Handeni road. I remember it as one of the show roads of the colony: broad, hard and clean. We found about two feet of dust on its surfaces:... dust that made of one colour all races of men, and gave us all one common cough 'to the pits of all our stomachs' as Kipling has it. And to the dust was added a stench that passes words: a stench now subtle and suggestive, now throttling and entirely disgusting; a stench that attracted one's gaze only that it might be repelled by visions of a sated jackal's half-eaten meal. For horses, oxen and mules have died by thousands.... Truly, war is hideous even at its base."[4]

Even in dry weather, a road would become utterly disgusting. The rotting beasts included those which had died on the march described by Brett Young, and by Angus Buchanan, an officer with the 25th Royal Fusiliers. The Bishop's vivid description continues:

> "Another agony of the road was its lack of water. I knew Zigualand from painful experience; but on my

arrival, I was given an official list of wells and watering places [made by the rains]. Twice did we resolve to halt where the Army said good water was, and twice did we repent ourselves of our trusting and confiding spirit. On the first occasion, it was midday and there was no water at all: only a vast camping place where water had once been The second day, we had marched nearly fifteen miles and wanted food. The so-called well was . a museum of dead frogs . It remained to do another six miles onward. And the man who has not had to do extra miles beyond his promised halting place, under tropical sun, has yet much to learn of what a broken spirit really means."[5]

This picture of the Handeni road, with its dust of death and empty wells, shows only too clearly the need for stringent water regulations in Force Orders, and also that carriers tended to suffer most if water was short simply because they arrived after the troops. "This was a commander's worst anxiety," wrote Major-General (formerly Colonel) Sheppard; and since streams were few in the dry season, his motto was: "Hunger is a trifle, but no water is death".[6] Smuts however, had no time for such realities. His view was that there were no such things as *hunger! and thirst!* when the success of a great operation hang in the balance. When an army used animal transport as well as carriers, the pressure on dwindling water supplies was even greater. Thirst probably finished off many exhausted men.

A later stage of the Handeni road, of which even the Army said there was no water at all, was done by night. An infantry officer, Captain Anderson, commented that troops had no option because during the day, lorries stirred up the dust which was a foot deep. His account agrees with Weston's about the rotting carcasses and befouled water holes.

Weston combines saintliness and prophetic insight with remarkable gifts of leadership. He understood a porter's work after many peacetime safaris as his account shows:

> "Of course porters do not move quickly. They have their own food etc. to carry as well as the official loads [perhaps made up to] 80 pounds, whereas the porter requires 50 pounds or at most 55 .so that most men must either carry overweight, or share a load that is not up to the two men standard and so waste the 'lift' of your column. The last lot of supplies I handled, very many thousands of loads, was almost entirely made of 80 lb bags, and 96 lb boxes of ammunitions."[7]

Watkins would have been very angry when Weston told him about this as he almost certainly did; but these large loads had probably been made up for mules, oxen, donkeys and carts drawn by animals. The beasts were now dead and the loads were impossible to divide. The Bishop was in a position to insist on improvements to the porters' lot. He argued:

> "They have to be rested otherwise men fall out and get lost or run away, or get overtired and ill. And to rest a column of 1,000 carriers in single file or at best in double file, takes time; with the result that two and a half miles an hour is very fast, and one and a half is unknown . the stronger men get in well ahead of the last men, whose job it is to urge on the tired, look out for dropped loads, and gather up the sick. If there be a more weary work than coming last of such a column

on a march of fifteen miles, I have not yet seen, heard or read of it. Yet it is not unuseful. Our men did very well on this particular work. We made a record for the journey both in time and accuracy. That is, we got our loads there quicker than other porters, and we got them all there. I gather this was not common".[8]

The above account is a valuable piece of evidence on the related questions of lost loads and carriers dropping out. In very severe conditions, as on the road past the Uluguru Mountains to the Rufiji, a carrier fallen out meant a lost load even if the exhausted carrier was put on a stretcher. A Luo witness, Yohana Ojwang, said that this was the practice in his time.

There were deaths from pneumonia, dysentery and cerebrospinal meningitis, a very dangerous disease which was especially common in Uganda. It would be interesting to know whether the pneumonia was due to the ghastly dust since respiratory diseases are often worst at the end of the long dry season. They returned to Korogwe and were joined by Johnstone, described by the Bishop as a real tower of strength and a most pleasant fellow worker. They were suddenly given two days to return to Tanga forty miles away to embark for Bagamoyo. Their column, about a mile and a half long, was led by Weston with Johnstone in the rear. They left at 4 p.m., torrential rain fell, and they followed the railway whose bridges consisted mainly of sleepers "not too close together". Johnstone was almost carrying night-blind men across, but although one man fell in a pool, none were lost. Only the fly sheets of tents could be put up and many men slept under a goods train, whose driver had to be told not to start until he had awakened them. Many fell sick and one long delay was caused by the column splitting into two, but after a better second night, they marched into Tanga at 7 a.m. singing lustily and happy. Weston wrote:

> "Marching at night is no joke, and it is no uncommon thing to fall asleep as one walks. Africans can go to sleep the moment they put down their loads, and need much persuasion to get out again."[9]

At Bagamoyo, the Bishop was put in command of the Coast Column Carriers. He was told to provide 2,500 men, but despite being given another 1,000, they were still a few hundred short. The answer was to commandeer all the two-and four-wheel carts in the town. Five men could pull a two-wheeler, carrying perhaps 500 lbs. Though some officers doubted whether the road would be suitable, it was carts or nothing since backs would not go round. Despite dust and a late start, they started well but a night march had to be made to catch up with the column. Soon after 1 a.m., they were stopped by the camp of the Supplies Officer with his staff blocking their path. A sergeant told the Bishop that the oxen were wind-broken, the porters back-broken and the staff heart-broken and that he had experience as a Catechist. He also said it was clear the moment for further questioning was not yet.

Supplies had to be taken through if the column was not to be rationless but for Weston, it was the great day of his life. The road was not suitable for wheeled traffic but with frantic labour, whereby porters carried 75 lbs each and a total of two and a half hours sleep in two days, the rations reached the front and the carriers were sent home for they were now redundant. Weston's heroic carriers also took over a naval three-pounder gun on a clumsy home-made chassis which they dragged for two days with their loads. An African witness told of his alarm when the Bishop fell trying to stop the gun going down a slope. Finally, "it was a very cheerful and grateful crowd that entered Dar-es-Salaam [sic] at the double with the gun rattling over the roads. The very rattle was welcome, telling of sand left behind and mud passed."[10]

They worked for a fortnight in Dar es Salaam as they had done in Tanga. Their camp was a little way out. An African witness whose name we do not know wrote:

> "The Lord Bishop loved the souls of his men and knew their weakness and so he was ever unwilling to camp very close to a town. He was also intensely busy with pastoral work, hospital visiting, and helping officers with native languages and difficulties."[11]

Then the Bishop and Johnstone left with a few hundred porters for the southern port of Mikindani, which like Dar es Salaam, Lindi and Kilwa, was taken in September 1916. They marched over a hundred miles inland to Masasi, an UMCA station. Weston rejoiced after he found it undamaged and its church being used as a hospital. However, bitter fighting was to take place there a year later. They returned via Sudi and Lindi to Kilwa Kisiwani, where Richardson joined them in the hard work of unloading troops and stores. Finally, as Weston was taking porters to the Rufiji, he was seized by a high fever. He was put on a boat to Zanzibar where he refused to land without his men. He had to think, he explained, of the relatives of his porters and of the rumours which would spread directly if it was known that he had returned to Zanzibar without his men. So he returned to Dar es Salaam to collect them. The same unknown African wrote that those who were not of Zanzibar cried for the

Lord Bishop, and that there was great lamentation.

Meticulous military efficiency was combined with inspired Christian leadership. Said our witness:

> "All the men obeyed every word of the Lord Bishop without question, not because they were afraid or because they were forced, but because the Lord Bishop treated them as a father does his children".[12]

There were troubles, but they were few in number. Johnstone said that discipline was the most rigid he had known and that when the Bishop once decided a thing was possible he spared no one, himself included. He also said that the only theft which seemed to have occurred resulted in a more severe beating than he (Johnstone) could have imposed. He wrote:

> " I am sure, however, that he was right, for such a thing never happened again. He ceased for a time to seem like a churchman and became a soldier; I am sure he felt that, by doing his work, he was setting a guide to others who were to follow."[13]

A medical officer's report on the men who returned to Zanzibar says:

> "It was very pleasant to see in what good condition they were. This was due to the great care that the bishop had taken of his men. He had seen that they were properly treated and this, I regret to say, was not always the case."[14]

In telling transport officials at Korogwe and Bagamoyo his opinion of oversized loads, Weston had the immense advantage of knowing what men could carry in such a climate, for how long, and what food and rest they needed. We are not told about their rations, but their good health at the end of their service suggests that they were well fed.

The Zanzibar Carrier Corps did not, fortunately, take part in active operations. The three mission officers served without cost to the military. Weston agreed that Baker and Richardson could continue to serve after the end of their engagement provided that they were properly commissioned and put on pay lists like military officers. Later, he complained privately to Watkins that Major-General Ewart (Adjutant and Quartermaster-General) accused him of wrongfully withdrawing the laymen. Lamented Bishop Weston:

> "It seems to me a very painful suggestion that my provision of a staff for ZCC free of charge to the military should be taken by GHQ as a basis for a claim for the permanent services of my staff after ZCC ceases to exist."[15]

General Headquarters' side of this is not known, but on the face of it, they had behaved in a most insulting and ungrateful way. The Bishop thanked Watkins warmly for his kindness to him at all times. Watkins' preservation of the Bishop's letter implies strong sympathy with Weston at the gaucheness of their military superiors. Weston's mental exhaustion can be read into this distressful letter ... "it just spoils all the pleasure we have had and creates a barrier against pleasant memories of our work."[16]

The cordial relations between Weston and Watkins shown by this letter are evidence of long talks in Dar es Salaam about Weston's practical experience of carriers on the march. Weston's views and experience would have given Watkins a battery of powerful arguments to use in the struggle to improve the working conditions of the carriers.

Bishop Frank Weston concludes his story: "I can only add that we really enjoyed our work, and that it was more exacting than any of us had met before, and that I am exceedingly sorry I could not see it through to the end."[17]

The Uganda Carriers

Atalukugendere akusibidde etanda y'amanvu (Luganda proverb: He who will not accompany you on the journey has given you ripe bananas)

Uganda carriers played an important part in the operations up to the Central Railway. After the occupation of Tabora, they were less noticeable until the mass levy of 1917 revived the vexed question of their employment far from their homes.

The Ganda, Soga and other people living to the north of Lake Victoria ate many kinds of bananas as their staple diet, especially *matoke* (plantains) which are cooked, but can also be made into flour. Bananas do not last long, which makes them most unsuitable to take on a journey, as the above Luganda proverb explains. They also have in their skins a high proportion of wasted weight. People so dependent on food usually eaten "green" off the tree tend to suffer more severely from a sudden change to any kind of grain. But grain flour itself can cause diarrhoea and dysentery even to "grain eaters" unless very carefully prepared. Dietary problems, serious enough with any porter, were therefore worse with Uganda men, except perhaps those from the Eastern Province who were grain eaters.

Earlier, we recounted the tragedy of the Uganda caravan of 1899. The Chief Secretary, H.R. Wallis, wrote after the war:

"Uganda natives, unless carefully dieted and accustomed to rice and flour for a considerable period beforehand, cannot be successfully employed away from their own country... when so taken, a terrible mortality has resulted from intestinal diseases. Once they become accustomed to strange foods, they render excellent service, but the proportion which can be so used is very small."[18]

In 1914, a contingent of 3,576 Carriers was sent from Uganda to the East Africa Carrier Corps. In Uganda, both people and officials may justifiably have felt anxious. Their worst fears were realised. Sir Frederick Jackson, the Governor, complained bitterly in June 1915 that while 722 had been repatriated and 2,000 were still serving, 854 had died or were missing — a death rate of 23%, after serving, under conditions which had called forth protests both from the Administrative Officers in charge and the Medical Officers. Apart from desertions, other major causes were unsuitable diet, malaria and other sickness, and separation from their officers who knew their language and customs: the problem of control again. This had caused alarm among the people, unequalled since the disaster that befell those porters who took down the Indian battalion from Uganda in 1899.

In 1915, there had been a sharp difference of opinion between the Carrier and medical staff on the one hand, and the settler-dominated Central Committee of Supply (CCS) on the other, about the quality of maize and *wimbi* (millet) meal issued to the men. The cause of the dysentery epidemic among carriers was attributed by E.L. Scott, the Uganda officer who was Watkins' chief adviser on rations, to unsifted *wimbi* flour milled at

Kisumu. After three months, 40% of the men had to be invalided home. The findings were handed to the military staff in November 1914 and should have been final but Major-General Stewart dismissed Scott's verdict claiming it lacked evidence, and ascribed the dysentery to want of ordinary sanitary precautions. No doubt he was listening to biased local opinion, particularly the pseudo-experts of the CCS rather than to administrative and medical officers who knew the facts. Admittedly, the death rate among *wimbi*-fed carriers on the Kagera front declined at that time, but the evidence for the lethal effects of dirty or unsifted flour was overwhelming.

Here follows three examples of suffering among Uganda carriers which are relevant to the Carrier Corps as a whole. They all involve water transport. Two are shocking instances of what usually happened when carriers were outside the control of their own officers, and were completely unsupervised.

The first example is about a man named Kasoga who was a porter of Chief Kimbuya of Kisonga. He died on board *HMS Nyanza,* while bringing 500 carriers from Karungu in South Nyanza. The medical officer at the Civil Hospital at Entebbe reported in March 1915:

> "A rag of barkcloth was apparently his only personal effect. The body was in a state of extreme emaciation, the whole alimentary tract empty, the intestines and visceral peritoneum acutely inflamed, and the mucous membrane covered with ulcers. In my opinion, death was caused by acute dysentery and lack of treatment."[19]

Forty others were ill. Five were expected to die. No one was in charge of the wretched porters overcrowded on the deck and exposed for ten hours to wind and rain. The ship's officers were said to have been unaware of their appalling conditions, which sounds a little hard to believe.

The second incident was in February 1916, when the Uganda Carrier Section was taken over by the Military Labour Bureau. Unaccompanied by any officer, 88 recruits travelled for two days by open lighter and train from Masinde on Lake Kyoga to Jinja, where they boarded *SS Usoga* to Sango Bay in the south of Lake Victoria. Their food was a mass of precooked *wimbi* and beans, dumped uncovered on the lower deck, where it decomposed. It made 70 carriers fall sick, out of whom 15 died of ptomaine poisoning.

The third example led to an enlightening enquiry. Miss Buxton was a European settler at Kericho. Her syce was convicted of theft, and conscription into the Carrier Corps was suggested. She replied: "I cannot consent to let any of my boys go into the Carrier Corps, after the awful way in which they are killed at Kampala. Seven a day are dying of starvation owing to having been six days without food at all."[20]

A Court of Enquiry found no evidence to justify what they termed a "sweeping statement" from Miss Buxton. It was concluded that she had evidently seen HMS *Sibyl* arrive at Kampala from Namirembe Bay with 700 carriers, 500 of whom were of the Belgian Congo Carrier Corps or Carbels, which were of Uganda men in Belgian service, while 180 were patients from Namirembe Hospital. Captain E.G. Fenning, commanding Carbels, told the Court that although they had been short of food, none were starving, nor had any died from starvation during the unit's existence. The Belgians had looked after them well, and had given them a fair allowance of food. The medical officers said that though this batch was worse off than most, deaths were due to dysentery and pneumonia, not starvation. They were received at Mengo Hospital, near Kampala, founded and run by Dr. (later Sir Albert) Cook of the Church Missionary Society (CMS) in 1897. His wife, Mrs. Katherine Cook, the Matron, said that the men had "wolfed" their first meal of soup and *matoke* without first washing their hands, which they were usually particular to do. Dr. Cook thought that Miss Buxton had mistaken dysentery patients for half-starved men (a natural error); green food eaters were so averse to strange foods that it was extremely difficult to get dysentery patients to eat enough. Dysentery patients cannot assimilate food, as the autopsy on Kasoga showed.

This affair showed both the difficulty of feeding Uganda carriers, and the efforts made to overcome the problems and to succour repatriates, in which Mengo Hospital played a big part. During the advance on Tabora in the second half of 1916, a growing stream of porters returned across the Lake, including those seen by Miss Buxton. On 19th July, Dr. Cook was warned of 329 men returning from Namirembe on HMS *Nyanza*, and was asked how many he could accommodate at Mengo. Mrs. Cook replied, "Dr. Cook asks me to say that all 329 can be put up tonight."[21] These convoys arrived twice or thrice a week at only a few hours' notice, and would always be met with great coppers of hot soup, arrowroot gruel, thickened milk and *matoke* which along with the careful nursing which the men received, saved many lives.

Early in the war, a Uganda Stretcher Bearers Company was founded by boys of the CMS High School, Mengo, with students of the Government Medical Training School as instructors. The schoolboys proved superior to peasant recruits at stretcher drill, nursing and first aid, and the company became the Uganda Native Medical Corps, 150 strong. It was encouraged by the Kabaka of Buganda, Daudi Chwa, and the Katikiro, Sir Apolo Kagwa. Being mainly Ganda, the men could not be classed as followers, below the askari of other tribes, so they were called troops. They were disbanded after the fall of Bukoba in mid 1916, but their work had been so good that a new African Native Medical Corps was started in March 1917, commanded by Major Keane, Royal Army Medical Corps, and Captain Tomblings, a Uganda District Officer. All high school boys of over sixteen joined it, including many who had previously served. A cousin of the Kabaka, Prince Joseph Musanji, served as a lieutenant. They worked mostly at the Carrier and Sewa Haji Hospitals in Dar es Salaam, while Ganda NCOs were in charge of subordinate staff at many hospitals in German and Portuguese East Africa. The UANMC made an immense contribution out of all proportions to its small numbers.

Even this carefully organised unit suffered a high death rate with sixteen deaths before they left for German East Africa. This was largely due to an epidemic of spotted fever (cerebro-spinal meningitis). This lethal disease was very prevalent in Uganda, and its virulence is shown by the shocking death of one of Cook's colleagues, Dr. W. Hillbrook, who was bitten on the hand by a patient. Up to 1916, it was second only to dysentery as a cause of death among Uganda servicemen.

In December 1916, the Carrier Section and Carbels were disbanded. In March 1917, John Ainsworth, the East Africa Protectorate's leading expert on labour and PC Nyanza province, was appointed Military Commissioner for Labour with the rank of full colonel. He was to direct a mass levy of carriers in the East Africa Protectorate, Uganda and occupy enemy districts. The military wanted 120,000 porters for the 1917 offensive. Smuts had failed to defeat the Germans who were holding out in the difficult south-eastern corner of their territory. To finish the war, 120,000 porters were required. Jackson was about to retire and hand over to Wallis as acting Governor but both men were strongly opposed to demands for more porters, even from the grain eaters of the Eastern Province.

Labour recruitment was more organised in the East Africa Protectorate than in Uganda, mainly because of political pressure from settlers. In Uganda, the main cash crop was cotton grown by peasant cultivators, and political stability depended on the Buganda Agreement between the British and the Government of the Kabaka. The heavy mortality among carriers therefore made further recruitment a very delicate issue for British officers in all areas. Jackson was one of the pioneer administrators. A legendary character of great charm, he had been severely wounded in the Sudanese Mutiny. In December 1916, he rejected Smuts' requests for porters. Apart from the risk of their carrying plague, meningitis and smallpox, it was his opinion that it would have been little short of wholesale homicide to send men from arid areas, like the Eastern Province, to swampy ones, like the south east of German East Africa. This view was supported by the doctors. There is therefore, no doubt that Jackson would have entirely agreed with Wallis' attitude to the military demands.

Ainsworth, Watkins and a staff officer went to Entebbe, where they conferred on 28th March 1917 with Jackson and Wallis.

A Carrier Hospital, run by the Uganda African Native Medical Corps (This photograph is also in G.J. Keane and D.G. Tomblings, *The African Native Medical Corps)*

Courtesy of Dr. Clive Irvine

They agreed to recruit only from the Eastern Province, but Jackson and Wallis had other fears: it would conflict with KAR needs and cotton growing, which was a vital war material, not only for clothing and equipment, but also for stabilising the high explosive filling for shells and bombs. Though the German Lake districts had a large population, recruiting took too long because they were loosely administered compared to districts in Uganda or the East African Protectorate.

Census figures suggested that the Eastern Province of Uganda could produce an initial draft of 15,000 carriers, to be followed by another 1,500 a month. At the end of June, Wallis reported that about 6,750 out of 24,000 had been passed as fit. Recruits came in from Bakedi, Toro, Lango and Gulu Districts to Mjanji Depot on the Lake, where Mr. H.B. Thomas, of the Survey Department was serving as a Carrier Officer. Mr. Thomas became a distinguished historian of Uganda. In a letter to the author, his description of the inspection carried out by Dr. Wynstone Waters, a veteran medical officer from Seyidie, confirms Wallis' statement about the high rejection rate:

> "His examination of the porters... was to walk down the line of parade and, with a fly-whisk, indicate those unfit. I'd guess that two out of three were discarded. An outbreak of cerebro-spinal meningitis caused more losses. I've no notion how many were actually shipped across to Kisumu. By August, the flow from up-country was coming to an end and Mjanji depot began to fold up."[22]

Ainsworth had reason to be sceptical, perhaps. Nyanza had 86,759 men available, compared with the Eastern Province's 92,372. Yet it had produced 60% since the outbreak of war, compared with the Eastern Province's 9%. He also thought the attitude of the Uganda authorities was grudging, compared to the willing cooperation of those of the East Africa protectorate where he had to admit, however, that the levy was unsettling people, and that there was a shortage of fit men. Privately, he told Watkins that the poor physique of the recruits had been a revelation to him and that, the supply of the class of men required was nearly exhausted; but it is very unlikely that men who had only been home for three months would have been fit enough for further duty.

The plan for 1917 had been the work of Smuts' successor, General Hoskins. For political reasons, he was soon replaced by General van Deventer, who would not accept Wallis' explanations. Ainsworth and Watkins both had the problem of reconciling their political and military roles. Watkins was doubtful as to whether carrier quotas could be reached, just as the furore against Wallis was developing. In a report to Brigadier-General Fendall on 30th June 1917, Watkins referred to his previously stated opinion that, with all the commitments, wastage and medical rejection rate, labour would not be available to carry out the original plans of General Staff. There was no suggestion that the Uganda government was to blame for the result of over ambitious military planning, even if their recruitment figures did not compare well with those of the East Africa Protectorate.

General van Deventer's case against Uganda was that civil officers failed to recognise how urgent the military need was for porters, and that the chiefs were withholding able bodied men from medical examination, which Wallis said was unjust and uncalled for. The Colonial Office took van Deventer's side and demanded an explanation for the rejection rate of 88%, compared with that of 45% in the East Africa Protectorate. Wallis replied that out of 102,000 men aged between 16 and 60, 42,000 were called up and only 7,500 accepted. He was told to explain this or stand convicted of bad faith and passive resistance.

Wallis was retired in 1918. He died in 1946. Paying tribute to Wallis' competent handling of the unprecedented emergency in 1914, H.B. Thomas wrote of the man:

> "H.R.W. was hard-bitten and forthright with long experience of Africa. He had every reason to stand up to the military [who] broke him in the end, but it will be no service to the memory of a high-minded and selfless public servant to suppress the fact that Mr. H.R. Wallis retired and died a disappointed man."[23]

Wallis thought that military demands on Uganda's manpower were ill-considered, and the losses from illness fearful and was not afraid to say so. No further civil promotion was offered to him, and he was refused a knighthood. It is very doubtful whether Sir Frederick Jackson, who would have taken just the same line, would have been treated as Wallis was.

Making Wallis a scapegoat, like the replacement of Hoskins by van Deventer, was apparently to appease the South Africans. The Military Labour Bureau total for 1917 was actually 11,936, not 7,500. The reason for this discrepancy is not known, but the conclusion here is that Wallis had been very badly treated.

The Kikuyu Mission Volunteers

Surely your God is a God of power, and he has cared for you and returned you to us safely
Inland Africa, August 1918. (By courtesy of Dr. J. Forbes Munro)

"Ni guteithania turateithania" (We are only helping out) was a comment frequently made by members of the Kikuyu Mission Volunteers (KMV). During their short life as a unit, from April to December 1917, the KMV probably developed a greater pride in themselves than any other part of the Carrier Corps, except the Zanzibar carriers. Many of our witnesses had served with the KMV, and were obviously proud to have done so.

The KMV was a contribution to the mass levy of 1917 jointly made by the Church of Scotland, the Church Missionary Society (CMS), the Africa Inland Mission (AIM), and the Gospel Missionary Society (GMS). It was based on the pre-war ecumenical movement of Protestant Churches in East Africa which led to the conference in 1913 at Thogoto, the headquarters of the Church of Scotland in Kikuyu. One of the founders of the "Kikuyu ideal" was the Rev. Dr. John W. Arthur. He was the leader of the KMV; a man of action, a mountain climber and rugby player. as well as a doctor and minister of the Scottish Church.

When war broke out, missionaries shared the general view that it was "business as usual." The war would be settled in Europe. In 1916, however, a hospital for carriers returning from German East Africa was opened at Kikuyu. By 30th June, 161 patients had been admitted, of whom 78 had been discharged. In 1917, the mass levy meant that all Europeans also had to register. The Rev. H. D. Hopper, of the CMS at Kahuhia, saw an opportunity for raising a special force for mission followers, who would otherwise have to join the regular Carrier Corps. The moral effect of such a venture would be valuable, and it would give them a chance of sharing the general hardships. To government officials and others, it would be a striking refutation of the commonly repeated story that mission schools were the refuge of all the able-bodied loafers, because many had sought refuge from conscription at the missions. Hooper learned from Archdeacon Hamshere that Arthur had a similar idea. It was approved by Colonel Ainsworth, Military Commissioner for Labour, and Lieut-Colonel Watkins, the Director of Military Labour.

The plan came as a relief to African Church leaders and members at Kikuyu when it was explained to them at a large prayer meeting. It was obviously preferable to the alternative of press-ganging, and within a day, 112 young men had joined: teachers, hospital orderlies, masons, carpenters and shamba workers. A Limuru man, Nathaniel Mahingu, had this to say; "When the Wagikuyu heard that the missionaries were going, and missionaries don't fight, very many of us agreed to go". On 1st April 1917, 1,800 carriers gathered at Kikuyu for a month's training. About half of the Kikuyu came from Murang'a district while about a hundred AIM men came from Machakos. Captain Arthur was in command and under him were: 2nd Lieutenants Hooper, from CMS; Barlow and Tait (both from Church of Scotland); seven Non-commissioned officers (NCOs) including five British; Whibley and Gray Leakey, both from CMS; Clarke, Stephenson and Guilding, from AIM.

According to the information gathered from Silas Kiige, Samwel Ngoci and Ishmaeli, all from Kahuhia, Leakey was called

Murungaru (straight man); Whibley was generally known as *Waitina* (Big Bottom), a peculiarity also recalled by Nathaniel Mahingu. There were three grades of headmen: one, those incharge of over 100 men; two, those over fifty, three, those over twenty-five. Tagi, a literate Maasai of the AIM and a trusted evangelist, was a superior headman while Samwel Ngoci was an overseer, perhaps of over twenty-five men. The story of the KMV is told in detail by John Arthur in his diary, and in his letters home to Kikuyu. He wrote about Tagi and two others:

> "There is none his equal in the corps, as he formerly had military training that fitted him admirably for his present duties ... Mutua of Machakos is headman of over 100 men, Mabiewa is headman of over fifty men."[24]

The one month at Kikuyu was occupied with basic discipline, and plenty of hard work. There were medical checks and injections, presumably including the new anti-dysentery vaccine. They were inspected by C.C. Bowring who was the Acting Governor, Ainsworth, the District Commissioner and chiefs, including Kinyanjui wa Gatherimu. There were some desertions, but on Saturday 12 May, they arrived at Mazeras — about eleven and a half miles from Mombasa — 1,656 strong

At first, Arthur was enthusiastic about Mazeras. The drainage and firewood supply seemed adequate, but it had been found unhealthy when the headquarters of 1st (Nyasa) KAR was temporarily there in 1905. Heavy rain made the black cotton soil sticky. The KMV built a permanent camp for 6,000 carriers. Old bandas were burnt, grass cleared, latrines dug and incinerators built. After a month's hard work and meticulous medical care, over 1,600 men from the highlands were acclimatized with only three deaths being recorded: one from dysentery, and two from what Arthur thought was tetanus caused by quinine injections. This was a remarkable achievement, considering that there were hundreds down with influenza, malaria, dysentery and even smallpox.

The men disliked Mazeras as several accounts from survivors show:

> "There were a great many mosquitoes," wrote Tagi, "and it was very, very hot. Many of the boys were sick with malaria fever. The local Duruma were discouraging too: 'Oh, you have come to a very bad place here, and in the company that came before you, very many died, and we think that before you leave many of you will also die'."[25]

Wangoto of Kirogo in Murang'a District reported violent diarrhoea: "We were attacked by dysentery (*gatema or murimu wa kuharwo thakame*)," said Kinuthia of Ngecha, "Then we saw many flies, which could make the grass lie down."[26]

The KMV were originally destined for Lindi but there was a change of plan, probably due to political representations to general headquarters. But Nathaniel Mahingu understood that the change was for health reasons, while Tagi heard that it was hot at Lindi, with "very many mosquitoes, and very, very many of the Kikuyu people who went there died".[27] Their destination was now the Dodoma-Iringa line. Arthur was much relieved: "Had we gone, as was first intended, to the coast regions and on column work, our casualties must have far exceeded [the final] 5.5%."[28]

It is not clear on what number Arthur based this percentage, but if it was out of the 1,656 who arrived at Mazeras, then 5.5% was the 91 men that died there. Writing to the Official Historian in 1936, Arthur said that of 1,750 men, 25 had died and 50 or so were left at hospitals on the way home and were never heard of again. Officially, 13,748 carriers were recorded after the war as missing or presumed dead.

On the last Sunday at Mazeras, the united communion service was attended by 105 Africans, showing how few converts there were among the KMV. They sent 96 sick back to Voi from Mazeras, and another 90 from Mombasa. On the ship *SS Montrose*, they were accompanied by 400 men of the African Native Medical Corps, very neat, clean and proud. Putties and caps would, thought Arthur, have improved the appearance of the KMV, but they were not issued to ordinary carriers. Earlier, Arthur had "a fight with supplies over the boys' food and soaps" — an example of the problems many carrier officers faced when trying to secure the rights of their men. They disembarked at Dar es Salaam on 8th July. Arthur met Watkins and Lieut-Colonel Hill, chief medical officer with the Carrier Corps.

At Dodoma, they were rejoined by Barlow, Hooper and three NCOS who had been sent to Lindi. General Hoskins had agreed that the KMV would be kept together, perhaps following pressure by the missions on the Acting Governor, C.C. Bowring. There were now 1,499 men: 90 headmen, 19 hospital orderlies and 1,390 carriers. They left in three detachments for Iringa to support the Belgian column. Arthur resolved, in future, to carry the sick along with him, having had to leave 84 at Dodoma. They went through a cooler, healthier country, with attractive beech-like forests, and reached Iringa on 27th July.

Arthur praised the arrangements for sick carriers, especially at Major Roberts' hospital at Iringa with these words: "His treatment of his patients could not be excelled in any mission hospital, and he has amassed a large quantity of statistical material that ought to prove of great value."[29]

The KMV were fortunate to be working on a line instead of in column, in a very well-run unit, in healthy country, and in an area from which war had receded. However, although at 6,000 feet above sea level, it was very cold at night--they were spared the horrors of the period before the mass levy, of the heavy rains on the Rufiji and as we saw earlier, they were also spared the fierce fighting in December 1916, in this very area.

There was squalor at Muhanga, the RC mission which was the KMV base. It may have been due to warfare as well as to the multitudes constantly passing through; but Arthur thought that the officer in charge could not be blamed, as he had too little labour to keep it clean. He was Lieut. Butcher, a layman with the Universities' Mission to Central Africa. Butcher had been a prisoner at Tabora where prisoners had been ill-treated, and on his release had joined the Military Labour Bureau.

The KMV arrived at Muhanga 1,158 strong. They were joined by 193 sick from Iringa and 250 others, some from Nyanza and Embu District. Some of the sick had been sent back to Voi from Mazeras. They included Josiah Munyaka Kivanguli, a dispenser who was later an AIM pastor at Kangundo, Machakos District. A Thogoto headman called Benjamin led a party of 37 who had come across country from Voi. Theirs was a grim tale. Some of the medical orderlies had been commandeered, but fortunately, they arrived at Muhanga later. Their *jembes* and knives had been taken from them en route. At Dodoma, a doctor certified 23 as unfit. When there and during the march, they were so brutally treated by kiboko-wielding white NCOs of the Supplies Department that when they reached Iringa, many were at once put in hospital by Major Roberts. Reports Arthur,

> "Of the 117 boys who left Dodoma, only 50 got to Muhanga. This sort of thing I am afraid is not uncommon [Roberts agreed]. The chief authorities never hear about it as there is no one to take the boy's side or listen to his story."[30]

Arthur spent 1st September with a "ghastly" sick parade till noon, and wrote a report to the Director of Military Labour. One can only hope that Arthur and Roberts were able to give Watkins enough evidence to ensure that the men, whose barbarity had put over 100 carriers out of action, got the punishment they deserved.

While the KMV were supporting the Belgian advance on Mahenge, they were based at Muhanga, with an overspill at Boma Mzinga (Big Gun Fort), where Hooper was in charge. They started work on 2nd August and for the first month, it was very wet, sickness rife, and there was not enough labour to dig adequate latrines. There were 43 cases of dysentery, 160 of chest infections, and 378 of malaria, most likely contracted at Mazeras. Their health benefited from a football pitch which they made, and also from frequent games. Muhanga camp was finally condemned, and a new one was finished on 12th November. There had been 13 deaths and hundreds of sick since they arrived there but this was nothing to ordinary carrier experience, nor to what they would have suffered at Lindi. Except on 5th and 6th August, the pressure of work was so

A group of East Africa Protectorate Carriers
Courtesy of Dr. Clive Irvine

great that in practice, it was never possible to rest 33% of the men; even cooks and headmen had to carry loads.

Arthur describes the dumping or relay system between Muhanga and Mahenge quite well. He says that such hilly country posts could have been only seven miles apart, depending on supplies of water and firewood. That the KMV had brought loads of salt and food from Iringa, 41 miles from Muhanga. The first 30 miles to "Observation Hill" was covered by ambulances and lorries, the next four to Magazine Hill by donkeys. Carriers took loads on to a dump half way to Muhanga, which was seven miles on. So the KMV at Muhanga had a round trip of 14 miles to collect these loads. Boma Mzinga was six miles on; then the road fell steeply to the Kilombero valley, and on to Mahenge, which the Belgians took on 9th October. Arthur continues to say that while the *C* Company made camp, *A* and *B* Companies took over loads from the Magazine Hill porters, bore the loads past Muhanga and handed them on to the Boma Mzinga men. He writes:

> "They began with a double lift of 640 loads: 320 loads back + 480 forwards = 800; 480 forward + 400 back = 880. The line closed in late November, when countless numbers of bags of mealie meal, rice, sugar etc. and tins of oil which had been painfully carried forward over these ghastly hills were now taken as painfully back, and in addition to innumerable odds and ends."[31]

During the advance, return loads were mostly the sick and the wounded. KMVs usually carried stretchers back to the Magazine Hill dump and returned with food and ammunition.

Samwel Ngoci and his friends at Kahuhia remembered this relay work well, as did Kaniaru and Nathaniel Mahingu, who said:

"We took loads of bullets and then carried them to those people whom we met, and then they took them and carried them about twelve miles away. When Mahenge was captured, the bullets we were carrying were the same bullets which were used to defeat the Germans."[32]

To the missionaries, the KMV was an opportunity to carry out evangelism among ordinary carriers, and to bear witness to their faith. Arthur had the task of keeping alive the "Kikuyu vision" of mission federation. Inevitably, he had to deal with friction among his officers and NCOs of different churches, which could have been worrying, but Arthur's diplomatic gift was equal to the task.

Arthur saw the KMV experience like this: Missionaries and their followers were enriched by their fellowship and wandering in the wilderness. Their experience of army life-discipline, hygiene, the sea, new countries, different people — all would help to train leaders for the future African Church. They could work towards this through the monthly united communion service, and evangelism. This was carried on both in the KMV and among attached personnel, like some men from Kenia Province, who joined Hooper's party at Boma Mzinga (One of them recognised Daudi, a KMV headman who had worked as a teacher in Wimbi). Finally, in all that they had done, learned and undergone, there could be seen evidence of God's preserving power.

Tagi agreed with Arthur and remembered that they had gone away amid the doubts of their neighbours. He enthused: "God has power to care for His children, for they have trouble just as we do."[33] But they rejoiced, confident that God would lead them out and bring them back. Their obvious well-being and happiness, as when they marched singing through Iringa, impressed all who saw them. When they returned, their neighbours said: "Surely your God is a God of power, and He has cared for you and returned you to us safely".[34] Many of the KMV found, on their return, that their relations had not shared their faith, presumed their deaths and divided their property. Their safe return caused much embarrassment.

Those who survived agreed that they had been very fortunate. The Kahuhia men said that ordinary carriers were liable to be badly treated, but not the KMV, because they were under missionaries. Nathaniel Mahingu, a Kahuhia man, had this to say:

> "We were well looked after. Even the nurses were ours; we had come with them from Thogoto. And Dr. Arthur was a nurse too! The government had said that we should never be taken to a place where there was fighting; it had rather we die of disease than from being shot.... I wish you saw how people were as fat as hippos when they were coming home."[35]

With religious enthusiasm and dedicated leadership, KMV morale was very high. Mahingu mentioned the weekly prayer meetings, and others spoke of hymn-singing. "We only sang Christian songs when it was allowed or during prayer time," said Mwova Kataka, a Machakos carrier.[36] Wangoto, from Kirogo in Murang'a District, repeated a hymn: *"Advance in happiness, because it is God who has directed thus"*. Prayer meetings were compulsory for all, even for the opportunists who had joined KMV to escape the regular levy. Kaniaru, who was a bugler, said that religion was mostly learned in the war.

Morning prayers were impossible after they left Mazeras, but every morning, shortly after the bugle went at 5.50 am, the sound of the morning hymn could be heard rising from the huts all over the camp, They would gather for prayer and scripture readings whenever possible during the day. After sundown, the superior headmen took evening prayers and hymns with an address. The few Roman Catholics repeated Latin prayers and also recited their rosaries. The Sunday service was that of the Federation; for instance, at Muhanga, there was no such thing as denominations, but a united band of Christ's followers worshipping Him as their one King and Lord.

There were comparatively few deaths, and their faith gave them strength to bear it when it came. In Elspeth Huxley's novel *Red Strangers*, Reri, the main character, is caught in the mass levy. He tells a tale of unrelieved horror. Especially terrible is the idea that a dead man's spirit can never find rest far from home and clan. Yet, the Luo and the Kikuyu whom we interviewed, like the Luo gun-carrier Okech Atonga, tended to agree that the living were too concerned about their own predicament to worry much about the spirits of the dead for whom they had no time to perform proper rites anyway. Mahingu's friend, Kinyanjui wa Mukura, was a carrier on the Rufiji where he saw some grim things; "Once your companion died, you were gripped with fear for the rest of your time there," he said, but quoted a Kikuyu proverb: *Mundu wa itimu ndari miarire* (a warrior can die anywhere). This seems a more comfortable philosophy than that of Elspeth Huxley's Reri. The Kahuhia men said: "We felt worried because of leaving our dead in a strange country, but we did not worry about their spirits because we were Christians".[37]

Some of the KMV mentioned contacts with people of the

countries through which they travelled. Josphat Njoroge avoided such meetings, but Silas Kiige, Samwel Ngoci and Ishmaeli, of Kahuhia, said they used to go visiting in the other camps and added, "We came to know each other very well when we learned how to speak Swahili, and we even visited native homes in Tanganyika."[38] They found that the Wagogo had similar customs to the Kikuyu except that they used dogs as part of the dowry price; and like the Kikuyu, they knew God but in their methods of worship they used foodstuffs, while the Kikuyu used animals for sacrifice. Silas Kiige, who was about 90 years old at the time of the interview and was commended by his friends for his excellent memory, showed us his fine hardwood staff which he had cut at Muhanga and which was still one of his most prized possessions.

A feeling of peace came over Arthur as they waited for news that the Dodoma - Iringa line was to close and on 21st November, they heard that it was closing. They burnt the old hospital and Kaisser in effigy. Arthur was relieved when an order to relay some stores back from Kaswaga in the Kilombero lowlands was rescinded as it would probably have meant 10% deaths . After heavy work returning stores down the line, they reached Dodoma. On 13th December, while hunting for water at Mwitihira, Arthur chanced to meet a young doctor of the Royal Army Medical Corps, Clive Irvine, who later founded and ran the Church of Scotland hospital at Chogoria in the Mount Kenya region and is widely remembered for it. From Morogoro 2,248 men marched to Korogwe from where they returned to Nairobi by train via Voi.

It cannot be denied that between mission ideals and African traditions, roots of future conflicts were gradually emerging. For example, while Muthandi, a chief's son, agreed with Arthur that female circumcision was wrong; Josphat Njoroge, a Kiambu carrier, said that at Mazeras, Arthur had told them to stop the circumcision of girls when they went home but they did not like his suggestion. As we shall see in chapter six, the experience of the Kikuyu Mission Volunteers included frictions and tensions which were to develop fully in the post-war world.

Notes

[1] Interview at Kahuhia, 29 May 1970.
[2] H. Maynard Smith, *Frank, Bishop of Zanzibar* (London: SPCK, 1926), 186.
[3] Smith, *Frank*, 192-193.
[4] *Central Africa*, 1917, 28-32.
[5] Ibid., 27-32.
[6] Public Records Office (London), Cabinet Office Papers 45/34, notes 22 July 1932.
[7] Weston, Frank, *The Serfs of Great Britain* (London: Universities' Mission to Central Africa, 1920), 32-35.
[8] Public Records Office (London), Cabinet Office Papers 45/30, Anderson to Colonial Secretary Nairobi, 11 March 1938; *Central Africa*, 1917, 31-32.
[9] *Central Africa*, 1917, 28-32.
[10] Ibid., 28-32; Smith, *Frank*, 197.
[11] Smith, *Frank*, 197;
[12] Ibid., 97
[13] Ibid., 199-200.
[14] Ibid., 197-200.
[15] Watkins Report, Weston to Watkins (private), 10 Oct., 1916.
[16] Ibid.
[17] Ibid.
[18] Public Records Office (London) Colonial Office 536/90/6006, *Handbook of Uganda* (2nd ed. 1921), chapter 21 "The Great War in Uganda 1914-1917" 356.
[19] National Archives of Uganda, Secretariat Minute Paper 4290. Jackson to Belfield, 8 June 1915 (Research project Archives - Dept. of History, University of Nairobi, War F/1/2).

20 Watkins Report, C.M. Dobbs (DC) to Ainsworth, 14 Aug., 1916.
21 Albert Cook, *Uganda Memories* (Kampala, 1945), 306-308.
22 H.B. Thomas to the author of this book, 19 Jan. 1970.
23 Obituary in *East Africa*, 14 March 1946 by H.B. Thomas; Wallis drew attention to his services and work on the *Handbook of Uganda* - Colonial Office 536/93/2764 and 90/6006.
24 *Inland Africa*, 1,9 (Sept.), 11-12; The author is grateful to Dr. J. Forbes Munro for copies of the extracts.
25 *Inland Africa*, 2, 7 (July 1918), 12; Dr. A.T. Matson writes that Mazeras was found to be unhealthy in 1905, when the Headquarters of 1st KAR (Nyasa) Reserve Battalion was tentatively based there.
26 Interview at Kahuhia, 29 May, 1970 and at Ngecha, 10 May 1970.
27 Arthur papers, Diary 26 June to 3 July 1917.
28 *Kikuyu News*, 64, Arthur's letter 17 June,; papers, Diary 26-27 May, and Kikuyu Mission Annual Report, 1918; *Inland Africa, 27 (July 1918), 12*.
29 Arthur Papers, Circular Letter No. 2, Muhanga, 5 Sept. 1917.
30 Circular Letter No 2., 5 Sept., 4; Diary, 29 Aug. - 1 Sept.
31 Arthur Papers, Diary: 2-10 Aug. 1917, letters to Kikuyu, 5 Sept. 1917 and 1 Jan. 1918.
32 Interview with Mahingu and Mukura, June 1969.
33 Postscript to Diary "The K.M.V.: Summaries."
34 *Inland Africa*, 2, 8 (Aug. 1918), 13-15: "More about God's Presence with the Carrier Corps".
35 Interview at Kahuhia, 29 May, 1970.
36 Interview at Ithamboni, Machakos, 3 Oct. 1970 (Kathuli).
37 Interviews with Mahingu and Mukura on 8th Nov. 1969; Okech Atonga on 26 August, 1970; Kahuhia men on 21st February, 29 May and 25 November, 1970. Also, see Huxley, *Red Strangers*, 283-285.
38 Interview at Kahuhia.

Chapter Five

Carrier Welfare

Rations and Medicines

*When we were in Maktau many carriers and stretcher bearers, who used to eat **maharagwe**, died because of this food*
(Muthyanya wa Muiri, KAR corporal, Kaaria age group, Meru)

Normally, anyone who falls ill after eating unusual food is certain of the cause, and in the instance quoted above, Muthyanya was right, though the consequences may not have been quite so serious. The dietary experience of most Africans before the great war was limited to what they ate at home.

In 1912, the Native Labour Commission examined the conditions of labour in the East Africa Protectorate. Chiefs, headmen, settlers, missionaries, doctors and government officers were emphatic that food, housing and medical care were inadequate. For example, Chief Kutu said that men suffered from bad water, unusual food, too much maize which was often bad, and a lack of vegetables. Europeans well acquainted with Africans knew that they needed both a varied diet and time to adapt to sudden changes in climate. Luo suffered from cold in the highlands, and Kikuyu caught malaria on the coast. Doctors like Norman Leys and H.R.A. Philp agreed that until medical services were greatly improved, the general efficiency of labour would remain low.

As Provincial Commissioner for Nyanza, which produced over

half the labour in the Protectorate. John Ainsworth was the leading authority. He and Oscar Watkins recommended a Department of Native Affairs, a body of expert opinion which would set standards in everything to do with African welfare, especially housing and diet.

Enough research had already been done by anthropologists, missionaries and government officers on the diet of East African peoples to refute the mistaken but persistent idea that labour could thrive on a pound and a half of mealie meal and beans daily. The Ganda and their neighbours were "green food" eaters, with many types of banana as their staple food, especially *matoke* which was cooked but could also be made into flour. A sudden change of diet could have horrific results, as the 1899 caravan disaster showed. They also had meat, fish and many different vegetables. The Kikuyu and Kamba also ate a varied diet of millet, maize and several vegetables. For meat, the Kikuyu stuck to domestic animals, but the Kamba liked game meat also. Beer, whatever it was made of, remained an important part of the diet of the country people.

In East Africa, the King's African Rifles showed the same reactionary attitude towards diet as the less enlightened settlers. In 1912, two companies of 2 KAR had to be disbanded at Serenli (in Jubaland) following heavy mortality from *beri-beri*, caused by heat, lack of exercise and an unvaried diet of rice. A medical officer who joined the KAR at this time, Dr. C.J. Wilson, was specially interested in diet. He proposed a new and varied ration scale, which was rejected as unnecessary because it was argued that maize has always been the food of the African. Maize was in fact a comparative novelty up-country; the Luo were beginning to turn to it from millet. By this time, the diet for the workers on the mines in South Africa and Rhodesia was many years ahead of East Africa. There, the need for a balanced diet was well understood. Consequently, mealie, beans, meat, vegetables, groundnuts, salts, beer and a pint of hot soup, coffee or cocoa after night shift were provided to the Miners.

Today, it is hard for us to believe that in 1914, military opinion fixed the duration of the campaign at three to six months, with outside figures of 10,000 to 20,000 carriers in all areas. Lord Kitchener was one of the minority who predicted a long war. When the campaign prolonged, all defence measures had to be improvised from the scratch.

A District Officer with the Uganda contingent of the new Carrier Corps was E.L. Scott, whose special experience with food rationing for labour on the Busoga Railway made him familiar with the main items of diet. The commonest types of millet flour were *mtama* and *wimbi*. Scott preferred *wimbi* to *mtama* or maize because it stored better. For cooked rations, beans were better than flour, especially mealie meal which ferments quickly. Sieves were standardized. Before, Nyoro carriers in four Uganda Carrier Corps had bought their own for sifting the flour, which they thought was too coarse for their health.

Scott thought *mhinde* and *mpokya* were the most suitable beans, as they could be cooked in 20 minutes as long as they were not more than six months old. They tended to go weevily in store, but could be treated with ash or spread in the sun. He partly confirmed Corporal Muthanya's opinion of *maharagwe*, called *bijanjalo* by the Ganda. It took too long to cook, and however well prepared, caused diarrhoea if over a year old. Another member of the Kaaria age group in Meru, M'Inoti wa Tirikamu, said: "We refused to eat *maharagwe* because it killed many members of the *Riungu* age grade who were working in Nairobi."[1]

"Bananas", said Scott, "were wasteful to transport as only half their weight was edible."[2] The same applied to sweet potatoes, but they and *matoke* could both be made into flour. Rice had to be soaked before issue. Coast porters were used to rice, but most up-countrymen were not, and may not have realised how dangerous it was to stuff oneself with half-cooked rice.

Coarse, dirty or gritty meal of any kind took a long time to cook and it caused gastric irritation leading to diarrhoea and dysentery. This was the basic truth which the medical and carrier officers had to force General Staff to realise. Cooking and feeding were linked with cleanliness and sanitation, as Dr. C.J. Wilson noticed at Namanga, where he was medical officer with the East African Mounted Rifles but later, he became their historian.

"Enteric fever" spread with the arrival of Nyanza porters. They were known to carry the dysentery bacillus. It was impossible to enforce sanitation, or prevent the pollution of streams. Dust and flies further spread infection. In camps like Bissell or Namanga, the spread of disease was encouraged by hundreds of porters fouling a wide area. The small pre-war hunting safaris, fed on meat, offered no comparison. They and the traditional caravans were mobile and did not use too much water.

In October 1914, the Senior Medical Officer at Voi reported a sickness rate among carriers which was both excessive and largely preventable. Dysentery was due to bad sanitation and an unvaried diet of mealie which often contained grit. Pneumonia was caused by the poor diet, exhaustion and cold. The officer suggested that the diet should be varied with meat and vegetables which generally, were readily available. Since porters were scattered about so much that their officers could not supervise them properly or obtain accurate returns, he warned that ill-fed, unsupervised carriers endangered the health of the troops. Wilson had given a similar warning.

Scott, now the Carrier Corps quartermaster, tested samples of mealie, *wimbi* and *mtama*. He concluded that : one ton in every six sent to Nairobi was a pure waste of transport; fresh grain had to be used, cleaned before milling and sieved before issue, as some men were already doing; and that, the waste had to be made good. Then the Central Committee of Supply was enraged, fearing a demand by civilian workers for better rations.

Watkins sent samples of flour to Ainsworth, with the comment, "We are up against the Nairobi mealie meal ring."[3] He was determined to refute their suggestion that the food was as good as the men would get at home. Writing to the Deputy Adjutant and Quartermaster-General, Watkins pointed out that the efficiency of carriers depended on their health, which meant giving them their accustomed foods. "We have to fight against a pernicious Nairobi tradition that unvaried mealie meal is the one food of all African natives," he argued.[4] Dr. Wilson also condemned "the folly and inhumanity" of this view.[5] The ration at this time was 1 1/2 lbs of flour, eight oz of beans and vegetables, 1/2 lb of meat (or beans if not available) and 1/2 oz of salt.

Next, Watkins wrote to the Senior Medical Officer Nairobi, with copies to Ainsworth, the Chief Secretaries in Nairobi and Entebbe, and the Supply Officer Mombasa. For military, political and humanitarian reasons, it was vital to prevent the recurrence of tragedies like the 1899 Uganda caravan or the Nandi campaign. Medical opinion attributed dysentery to food as the following comment from the Senior Medical Officer Voi shows, "The Committee of Supplies will see the absurdity of appointing expert advisers merely to ignore their views."[6] He also reiterated the superiority of African home cooking and the difficulty of cooking in the field, "To say that food needs long cooking is to condemn it for military purposes."[7] The Officer was supported by the SMO Carrier Corps, who thought that the attitude of the Committee was a matter for regret, and also by the Government Analyst who pointed out that samples of flour tested at Kisumu were too coarse.

Though the Carrier Corps lost the battle with the Committee of Supplies, they won a better diet and the use of sieves. A new South African medical staff arrived in 1916 led by Major Ernest Hill, who became SMO with the Military Labour Bureau and brought in extra daily rations. These were: 2 oz of potatoes, plantains, bananas or sweet potatoes; 2 oz jaggery or goor (Indian sugars); and 2 oz sim sim oil or two green coconuts weekly. Hill insisted that men in hilly, cold, sandy or swampy country, where the labour was heavier must have extra sugar.

It has been said that carrier mortality was the result of bad quartermastering. This is not true of the Carrier Corps quartermasters or their medical advisers, who knew what was needed and recommended it. The carriers were also dependent on the willingness of combatant units to share and share alike. The Belgians had done so, to their credit, with their Uganda carriers in the advance on Tabora. The 2nd South African Division at Iringa had acted otherwise, prompting protests from the Senior Carrier Officer and Captain Carnelly. The Supplies

Department may have had difficulties in providing the goods, but it is on record that they were often inefficient or worse.

Mealie meal was more easily obtainable from the East African Protectorate than from South Africa because of the shortage of shipping. By 1917 however, South African mealie meal was overtaking the East African one in quantity. It was also superior in quality. "Unless East Africans can contrive to attain the standard set by South Africans, they should drop out of the competition altogether," was Watkins' comment.[8] He recruited a professional mealie meal tester from South Africa, who condemned a batch of East African meal at Mikesse in September 1917 as unfit for human consumption.

It became clear that even the best South African meal ought to be used only at bases, like those at Dar es Salaam, where it could be properly cooked in large cauldrons. In practice, it had also to be used at depots and up-country posts, especially those on lines of communication. Scott concluded that it was impossible to cook mealie properly in the field, even under the best conditions. The finest white meal needed an hour and a half to cook but even then the Carrier MO condemned the result. With the enemy about, in bad weather and with no time to find water or firewood, food was often hardly cooked at all. Presumably, there was by now enough shipping to import Indian rice. Soaked and swollen before cooking, which took only half an hour. Indian rice became standard for all African Troops and followers in the field.

People everywhere tend to attribute illness to strange and disagreeable food. For example, Makau Nzibu, elder of Iveti, Machakos Districts, wrongly blamed jaggery for causing dysentery, rather than grain and flour: He said, "One of the troubles was rotten grain. We were also rationed jaggery in place of vegetables for our maize flour which caused dysentery among the people. They started dying".⁹ His dislike for dates was shared by other carriers at Ngechu, Kiambu District. Other Machakos men confirmed the problems of flour and the difficulties of cooking it. For instant, William Nthenge, stretcher bearer (Kiu), said that the doctor would condemn bad flour. Nguku Mulwa (syce, Muthetheni), said that damp flour caused dysentery, while Nzioki Wambua (KAR), Mutiso Kanzivei, and Mulei Nguyo, remembered abandoning cooking pots and putting out fires when the enemy attacked.

Dates were familiar only to coast people, and were issued as train rations together with boiled rice. Later, they were replaced by tinned meat and biscuits which were the British soldier's staple diet. Dates were also used as a substitute for meat, perhaps also for sugar. If men were given uncooked rations before a journey, they tended to cook and eat it all at once with fatal consequences.

African diet was thought to be deficient in fat. Ghee, the Indian clarified butter, was most popular, but was usually reserved for Indians. Coconuts were hated by up-country men and were thought by medical officers to be too indigestible. To produce oil, coconuts or sim sim were crushed by mills, driven by steam or even camels, as was seen at Mombasa by Lazaro Maende, a South Nyanza carrier. Men complained that sim sim caused diarrhoea when mixed with other foods, but Scott thought that what they really disliked was having their food cooked for them. The supply of meat was no problem on a column advance or on a line of communication, when transport animals were dying rapidly. Plenty of fly-stricken trek oxen were available on the

Handeni road, as documented by Dr. Dolbey, in his *Sketches of the East African Campaign*. He wrote that carriers ate the nearest derelict ox or horse. Otochi Onduko, a gun carrier from Kisii, mentioned eating game; but people interviewed near Thomson's Falls said that Kikuyu would never eat unclean food. Still, the KMV men at Kahuhia said that they learned to like fish. The German raid into the north in 1917 upset the meat supply, as well as carrier recruiting. It was therefore suggested that meat for carriers be reduced to three times a week. Watkins presumed that all other units were being reduced, and that the whole burden of shortage was not being put onto carriers.

When Hill heard of the veterinary practice in Nairobi of passing measly beef as fit for consumption by natives, he retorted, "That a Veterinary Officer should decide as to what disorders a human being may rightly be exposed is preposterous."[10] Measly beef eaten by men on their way to the front explained the high incidence of tapeworm, together with several other parasites, found by the medical officer, Dr. W.H. Kauntze, at the Nairobi Carrier Depot. The parasites were found among returning carriers, especially dysentery patients. The doctors therefore insisted that porters' meat be killed, inspected and issued the same way it was being for the rest of the garrison. The principal was that carriers were to be treated like the troops.

By 1917, the army's dependence on carriers was obvious, and the expertise of Military Labour Bureau staff was hard to challenge. Yet, this was still attempted. Major Hill insisted that it was his duty, not that of the Assistant Director of Supplies, Lieut-Colonel Dunlop, to accept or reject locally cut sugar cane because when carried for any distance, it bruised, fermented, and caused stomach trouble. Again, Hill and Watkins declared that it

Carrier Welfare · 159 ·

was for the local carrier officer to decide whether mealie cobs might be suitable, not Brigadier-General W.F.S. Edwards, the Inspector-General of Communications, who had wanted to buy some. The ration scale, Watkins pointed out, was based on South African experience. He argued:

"If I once agree that it can be altered ... without the formality of a reference to myself or the Medical Officers appointed as advisers to the Department, the whole fabric falls to the ground, and we are back on the bad lines of trusting to individual discretion in essentially technical matters."[11]

Where the welfare of carriers was concerned, therefore, the opinion of Watkins or Hill, who later became a Lieutenant-Colonel, must outweigh that of a senior officer. Watkins' request to be made a full Colonel would have given him extra authority which he badly needed, but it was turned down, despite the absurdity of an officer with such vast responsibilities being no higher in rank than the commander of a battalion of 1,000 men.

There were 776 Seychellese stevedores working at Kilwa who were withdrawn after losing 222 men from disease and inadequate diet, a mortality of 28%, the highest in Military Labour Bureau records. A protest signed by Desire Celeste and 214 others stated that they had been contracted to work at Dar es Salaam only. They not only wished to serve the British flag to their last drop of blood, but also expected to be looked after better. The military seem not to have honoured their agreement with these unfortunate men.

In 1914, there had been one doctor for each Carrier Corps of 1,000 men, but in 1915, there were not enough medical officers for the rising numbers of carriers. The breakdown of control resulted in their separation from their doctors as well as from their carrier officers. The only solution was for the Military Labour Bureau to have its own medical staff, but it was nor until November 1917 that Hill was finally able to prevent the transfer of medical officers from carrier hospitals to combatant units. By this time, every Carrier Depot had its Hospital.

"In all carrier hospitals", wrote Dr. Kauntze, "dysentery formed the cause of admission in at least 50% of cases, and led to one third or more of all deaths."[12] No treatment or precautions against infection seemed to help. It is no wonder that doctors welcomed a transfer to fighting units. Intestinal infections, including dysentery, caused 50% of all deaths, pneumonia and bronchitis another 12 to 20% especially among men from warmer climates, whereas highland men suffered from malaria. Smallpox and cerebro-spinal meningitis could also push up the death rate. Many who died from no apparent reason probably lost the will to live, a recognised cause of death. Though many carriers must have died of exhaustion and hunger, very few were killed in action.

Dr. Kauntze took charge of the Nairobi Carrier Hospital in November 1916. He and Dr. Pirie, Government Pathologist, decided that the dysentery was of the bacillary type. Helped by Dr. Ross, Director of Laboratories, he developed a vaccine which was used in a 1 cc dose on men from Ukamba, Kenia and Kisumu (who included Uganda men), up to March 1917. Thereafter, the mass levy porters were given a 4 cc dose. A total of 76,000 men were vaccinated. The vaccine was not effective against amoebic dysentery, which was common south of the Central Railway. This, and the relatively short immunity given

Carrier Welfare

"rievously earned money." A sick Carrier, with a tropical ulcer
Courtesy of Dr. Clive Irvine

by the vaccine, must account for the sharp rise in dysentery cases in mid 1917. Nevertheless, the vaccine must have kept the death rate down, and was shown to be effective when it quelled an outbreak of dysentery at Mbagathi Barracks in Nairobi. It was a remarkable feat to have produced such a vaccine in very difficult times.

The convalescent diet was similar to that used for the Uganda carriers at Mengo Hospital. To improve morale and give patients the will to live so as to return home again, beer was valuable. The aim was to send men home as soon as they were fit to travel, but not before. A porter returning to Mombasa Depot was sent either to the Carrier Hospital or to the Convalescent Hospital. An expert from Britain fitted artificial limbs to the disabled. Kinyanjui wa Mukura convalesced for four months at Nairobi before his release. Umoa Mbatha, who was very ill with dysentery, spoke highly of the convalescent diet at Nairobi. Marius Ng'ang'a Karatu became a hospital dresser whose job was escorting patients on journeys. His high opinion of hospital treatment was borne out by three KAR men: M'Laibuni (Meru), Mulei Nguyo and Kimumo Kitui (Machakos).

In 1918, the Spanish influenza epidemic came. In Seyidie, 40% of the population caught it, and 4,500 died. *Kimiri*, as the Kikuyu called it, must have seemed like a final visitation of God to the afflicted people. Death could follow only two days after the onset of the disease. In the Carrier Corps, by now much smaller than it had been, the death rate showed a brief but horrifying rise. This final calamity of the Great War touched all humanity and many millions died worldwide.

Two officers in-charge of Carriers

May I draw to your attention the fact that carriers are human beings and that officers in charge of carriers are responsible to their governments for their men?

The above complaint by Major W.R. Lyon sums up the duty owed by carrier officers to their men. Lyon was the officer commanding 8th Nigeria Carrier Corps of Captain Storage, adjutant of the 2nd battalion of the Nigeria Regiment. The statement symbolises the fundamental doctrine, developed by its staff since the corps was started, that carrier officers must retain control of their men. This was the basis of the system of carrier administration which made the campaign possible, but which depended on equally good administration in supply and combatant units. Here, we find evidence of gross incompetence, callousness and even dishonesty. Only two personal stories of carrier officers in the field have been available for this book; those by Captain Carnelly and Major Lyon. To some extent, we have also used the splendid accounts by Bishop Weston and Dr. Arthur. However, neither the Zanzibar Mission Carrier Corps nor the Kikuyu Mission Volunteers saw any fighting. As we shall see, both worked in conditions which though rough, were at least tolerable except perhaps, on the Handeni road. Their leaders were eminent and influential men, able to protect them against the worst military abuses shown by Arthur's story to have been common. Nevertheless, neither of these mission carrier corps met with anything comparable in horror to the ghastly experience of Captain Carnelly and of Major Lyon.

Captain J.H. Carnelly was a member of a European farming family who still live in Kenya. European farmers provided both the KAR and the Carrier Corps with many of their best officers. They spoke Swahili and understood Africans. All we actually know of Captain Carnelly as a carrier officer is through a report which he wrote dated 20th January 1917. It is about the appalling sufferings of carriers of the 2nd Division in the Iringa area, a subject already mentioned in the section on carrier logistics. This was where the KMV were to work several months later. Much has been said of the state to which the heavy rains had reduced the Rufiji and Iringa lines of communication. "The sufferings and casualties of this period from September 1916 to March 1917 will never be fully known," wrote Watkins in his Report.[13] Captain Carnelly's story vividly illustrates this grim statement.

Northern Rhodesia Police, one of General Northey's units which was advancing from the south-west, entered Iringa on 29th August 1916; but in October, a strong German column under Major-General Wahle, a retired officer serving under von Lettow, advanced from Tabora, and bitter fighting went on until the new year. In the same month, the Germans nearly succeeded in retaking Iringa, and Northey's troops had to fight hard to hold onto their gains.

Originally, the 2nd Division had consisted mainly of South African troops. It was commanded by Major-General van Deventer and had advanced from Namanga to Dodoma during 1916, relying on animal and motor transport. The effort had finished off nearly all the animals, due to the shortage of transport and supplies, and the exhaustion of its men. The division was therefore unable to advance far south of the Central Railway. It was not until December that van Deventer was able to push on to Iringa in order to help Northey to drive the Germans off the Southern Highlands. His division was reduced to a brigade: he had the 8th South African Infantry and the South African Horse, now dismounted. It was described by one of the Official Historian's correspondents as the least efficient of the South African units. There were also the 17th Indian Infantry and the 4th KAR. Desperate fighting continued over Christmas to dislodge a German force from the Dabaga area, south of Iringa in freezing, torrential rain.

On 22nd December, the day before this battle began, Watkins at Dar es Salaam received wires from the Senior Carrier Officers with the 1st and 2nd Divisions. Troops and porters with the 1st Division, near the Rufiji, were on half to two thirds the proper rations. The Senior Commission Officer Iringa said;

> "Porters with advance have been rationed for ten days. Ration works out at $1\frac{1}{2}$lb meal and $\frac{1}{5}$lb meat per day. Expect deaths, desertion and sickness to occur on a large scale as work will be heavy and porters cannot stick it on these rations. Meal coming forward from Dodoma is not in waterproof bags so expect much will be sour as rains become heavy."[14]

Watkins passed this on to Brigadier-General Fendall, the Deputy Adjutant and Quartermaster-General, with the comment that he desired to record his strong protest against the treatment being given by the 2nd Division to their carriers. A further wire from Iringa on 17th January 1917 ran:

> "Supplies here refuse to issue full weight meal etc. *They issue all bags as 50lbs though they average only 40 lbs* [Author's italics]. Please protest against this."[15]

Watkins did so:

> "This if true means that losses through leakage and theft are being made good at the expense of the mens' health, and we are compelled to sign receipts for what we don't get."[16]

He passed it to the Assistant Director of Supplies at Dar es Salaam with the comments that if bags only averaged 40lbs, it was quite wrong to issue as 50lbs. He asked the director to please take up the matter.

Action seems to have been taken to correct this abuse, but it is against this background that we are to understand Captain Carnelly's report on the full horror of what carriers were actually suffering under irresponsible officers. The only letter by him which we have is dated 20th January 1917. It was written at Dabaga, about 30 miles south-east of Iringa, to the Senior Carrier Officer at Iringa. It refers to a letter written on the 16th which, unknown to Captain Carnelly, was already missing. Carnelly gave three sets of figures showing wastage of carriers at the South African Horse Camp, with the forward column and among men with Sergeant Butcher, presumably the hapless lieutenant whom Arthur was to find trying to keep Muhanga Camp clean with too few labourers. Among 1,755 carriers for whom Carnelly had been responsible, there had been 33 deaths and 431 desertions.

Captain Carnelly wrote in his report that the hardships the porters had been compelled to undergo could not be exaggerated. He gave examples as follows: That there had been no full rations since the Column left Iringa, often only 1/4 rations. The marches had been long and arduous over difficult country. The weather had often been bitterly cold and wet; only some 400 of the porters were provided with blankets. The staff of one British officer and three N.C.Os, as pointed out at Iringa, was inadequate. The Column frequently extended over three or four miles of country.

Carnelly went on to explain that many loads exceeded the laid

Carrier Welfare

down scale of 50Ibs. These exhausted the porters and delay was caused by lightening them following a march protest. Porters falling out in the course of the march were given posho by an N.C.O. who brought up the rear of the column. They were then ordered to join up as quickly as possible - many did not do so and were classed as deserters. Rejects were each given a ticket by the M.O., collected in batches, given posho and a covering letter showing numbers, date, days rationed and were then ordered to return to Iringa.

Practically, all the porters lost their *Kipande* or had it destroyed by the rains. Although warned that their pay depended on the production of their own *Kipande*, a good number gave their *Kipandes* to one headman to carry. That caused hopeless confusion. The Singedda [Singida] of whom there were 387 and the Wanyarambi 368, now numbered about a score between them. This and Carnelly's concluding remark suggest that all the 2nd Division's carriers were recruited in German East Africa.

As an example of what these unfortunate men had to undergo, Carnelly gives some details of the march on the 24th. He writes:

> "The porters lined up at 5 a.m. after a bitterly cold and wet night without shelter for the majority. The march was continued until 7.30 p.m. in the dark and wet. No halt was given for the porters to cook though there were a number of stops. No food was available at this hour for porters or other troops. The position of the porters was on a ridge a few yards wide on which it was dangerous to move in the dark. Actually, three mules fell over and were killed. No information could be obtained about the position of the camp which it had been hoped to reach at any moment. At 4

p.m., I went forward from my position in the column to point out to the staff that the porters were exhausted and should be halted - I was unable to reach them until between 7 & 8 p.m. A message then came through that the column had halted."[17]

Captain Carnelly would make no comment on the treatment of these porters except to express the opinion that the result would be disastrous for further recruiting.

Major W.R. Lyon was a Sierra Leone District Officer who had served in the 6th London Regiment before being transferred without any consultation, presumably because of his obvious qualifications to serve with the West African Force in East Africa. He was with the Nigerian Brigade near Lindi for the bitter fighting in late 1917, when nerves must have been at breaking point. In September, he complained to the Adjutant, 2nd Nigeria Regiment, that carriers of his own 8th Nigeria Carrier Corps, the 7th NCC and the Sierra Leone CC had been overloaded, *had had no water after a six-hour march because the troops had had it all*, and that 200 of them had been sent back for more loads at 3 p.m., having been up at 4 a.m. (Author's italics)

He complained that it appeared carriers were considered as little better than animals, " May I draw your attention to the fact that carriers are human beings, and that *officers in charge of carriers are responsible to their governments for their men?"* [Author's italics][18] Major W.R.Lyon made it known that he would do all he could to help the rapid movement of troops, but he also pointed out that the treatment of carriers was by then, wasteful and short-sighted.

No answer is on record, possibly because Lyon's strictures

were unanswerable. The Nigerian Brigade must have known the regulations perfectly well, including a carrier officer's duty, plainly stated in the Military Labour Bureau Handbook, to see that loads were kept down to 50lbs. Yet, Captain Downes seems ignorant of such details in his book about the Nigerians in East Africa. After the battle of Mahiwa, from 16th to 19th October 1917, Lyon asked if company commanders could account for 39 carriers missing but not in hospital returns. Again, he regretted troubling these officers, but he had to maintain his records and his contact with his men. The reply was curt and unhelpful, nor did circulating the list reveal the whereabouts of many carriers. Lyon repeated his request for accounts of carriers from the companies to whom they were issued, as otherwise he could not make his returns to the Director of Military Labour. If this was done daily, replacements could be sent daily without altering ration strengths. Lyon was told that it was the duty of his British NCO to see to this, but he later told Watkins that whenever he sent the NCO, the carriers were never properly paraded. Difficulties and excuses were made.

It had been a time of hard marching and fighting, with much suffering and heavy loss of life, frustration and strain. A day came when Lyon was in charge of Mendi first-line porters from Sierra Leone, and all the Nigerian Ibo second-line carriers, to repair roads. The three Mendi headmen all spoke good English, and must have understood Lyon's orders to parade at 5.30 a.m. next day. The Ibo were ready, but the Mendi were drifting off in small parties. The headmen said that a native soldier had told them to do so. It was the last straw. Lyon gave two of the headmen 24 lashes apiece for wilful disobedience. One of them reported to his officer, 2nd-Lieut. Despicht of *C* Company, that he had not only been flogged but was also threatened by Colour-Sergeant Rushby if he complained. Lyon and Rushby, who said that he had been asleep at the time, denied this. Lyon said that Goba, the headman, deserved further punishment for lying. The second headman who had been flogged and a third who had not, had gone with ten carriers to friends in another column.

Lyon had acted impulsively. He was authorised to award up to 12 lashes, and only for men of his own company. He was very sympathetic towards the Ibo carriers. He commented that the Adjutant and other officers of the 2 N.R. did not appreciate that with such men as the 8 N.C.C., to obey an order was not at all an instinct. That to punish them was often mere cruelty as they did not understand what they were being punished for. They had, for example, carried loads all day. Their headmen had taken so long a time to divide their food that 'lights out' had arrived before they could cook. They were tired, and knew that if they did not eat they would drop on the road the next day. Consequently they made fires despite all orders, the moment the European's back was turned.

Fires had to be out at nightfall with the enemy about, even if the men had not eaten. They could not gather firewood and water, and cook mealie meal in much under two hours. Until rice became the official field ration on 27th October 1917, men usually ate their porridge half-cooked, risking diarrhoea and dysentery. Lyon understood this, but officers of the Nigerian Brigade apparently did not. Lyon felt less sympathetic towards the English-speaking headmen, from whom he encountered the most explosive of all provocations, dumb insolence.

Lyon could probably have reached an agreement with Despicht, but most unwisely, he laid himself open to his enemies in the

2nd Nigerian Regiment by referring the matter to the commanding officer, Lieut-Colonel Parr. This angered Despicht so much that he complained to Watkins. He had already resented Lyon's ignoring his authority by punishing his men, who had always worked well for him, and by reporting to Parr over his head. Parr told the Brigade Carrier Officer that Lyon was incompetent and unsuited by temperament for the performance of his duties.

This opinion was based on personal observation in camp and on the line of march, but Lyon objected that no instances were quoted. Secondly, there was an unsubstantiated accusation that successive Adjutants had found it difficult to do business with Lyon. This, he said, was because he had based his duties mainly on paragraph 19 of M.L.B. Handbook, which was the classic summary of the carrier officer's duty. Obviously, he and the Adjutant saw the carriers from entirely different points of view.

Answering the final charge that the carriers themselves would not work under him, Lyon commented that if that was the only instance, it seemed to him to be a somewhat slender proof especially as Lt Despicht had said the remaining 1 HM & 9 carriers were not with him. He stated that his carriers worked as well for him as for anyone else; that they certainly kept better health when entirely in his charge. He regretted exceeding his disciplinary powers but also said that his temperament had not been a disadvantage during his five years as a political officer in Sierra Leone. He suggested that instances be quoted of people being unable to work under him, or of duties not carried out. Since further correspondence on this subject was refused, Lyon chose to proceed with it through Military Labour Bureau.

Lyon had erred badly over the flogging and in upsetting

Despicht, but the impression remains of an officer sincerely devoted to the welfare of his men, and to the performance of his duties. He was meticulous with his correspondence, which has proved helpful to this book. He copied his letters in a very clear hand on various Army forms for lack of writing papers. Mr. John Say, who taught geography in Kenya, recalls Major Lyon as a pleasant, kindly man.

There are no signs of any similar clash between Carnelly and the South Africans of 2nd Division, but he certainly protested on the spot at the mistreatment of his carriers. In such circumstances, it might have been very difficult to avoid an acrimonious argument. Paragraph 19 of the Military Labour Bureau Handbook, to which Lyon had referred, included this warning: "Carrier officers should never allow themselves to be drawn into an altercation [but] in the event of a difference of opinion state quietly that they propose to refer it to the D.M.L."[19]

Lyon's anger over the mistreatment of the Nigerian carriers was fully justified, but he does not seem to have followed this instruction. At the first sign of trouble in September, he should formally have warned the Adjutant of 2nd Nigerian Regime that any further breach of General Staff orders on the treatment of carriers would be instantly reported to the Director of Military Labour. Maybe he did. We do not know. His messages to the Adjutant following the battle of Mahiwa were models of diplomacy. Then suddenly, he had to deal with a gross breach of discipline, which was too much for his overwrought nerves, and in his anger, he committed a serious error of judgement.

Lyon said that during those three terrible months, the wastage in 8th Nigeria Carrier Corps was 64%. On 9th September, there

Carrier Welfare

had been 22 headmen and 396 carriers, but on 9th December, only eight headmen and 142 carriers were left. These figures are borne out by the official death rate of 20.4% among the Nigerian carriers, and 16.1% among those from Sierra Leone. The wastage seriously reduced both the efficiency and the mobility of the Nigerian Brigade, which had also suffered huge losses in battle losing 528 of the 1,750 men engaged at Mahiwa alone.

Throughout the campaign, the discipline of the East African Force was bad. One symptom was the contempt for force orders about carriers, resulting in constant interference with their management, and in brutal ill-treatment. By describing so clearly and vividly some of the difficulties he had to contend with, Major Lyon joins Captain Carnelly in showing how cruel, stupid and incompetent the supply and combatant officers were in their dealings with carriers and how this reduced the fighting strength of the troops who were expected to defeat the Germans.

Wages and claims

The payment was a debt of honour incumbent upon His Majesty's Government to meet
(Leo Amery, Colonial Secretary, 1927)

Until the East Africa Carrier Corps was formed in August 1914, there was no military transport corps. The only precedents were temporary groups of carriers raised for the Nandi campaigns and similar operations. The Carrier Corps was started by officers who were civilians but were soon given military ranks. Wages paid to carriers competed with those offered to others locally. They varied from Rs. 4 or 5 on

Kiambu farms to Rs. 10 on the Uganda Railway, coast plantations, or Kilindini Docks. In Seyidie, carriers were paid Rs. 10 except the Swahili, who expected at least Rs. 12. Military service competed for labour with other employers, as no one thought that the war would last long. Hence, an offer of Rs. 20 for gun carriers produced only three men at Malindi. However, the PC Seyidie, Charles Hobley, warned that Rs. 15 was the minimum for volunteers.

Before pay rates were standardised, disputes were inevitable. Kamandu joined the KAR patrol as a carrier headman during the Giriama uprising. He drew Rs. 20 a month while a porter was getting Rs. 15, including food. He deserted in November 1914 because the KAR said they gave headmen only Rs. 15. Hobley was satisfied that Kamandu's record was good, and ordered that he be paid in full. Another headman, Nubi bin Safu, had been transferred from Surveys to the Machine Gun section in October 1914 and then to carriers at Rs. 20. He claimed that he was owed Rs. 69.61. Nubi's claim was corroborated by the DC Mombasa who said that he heard of such cases daily. It is not surprising therefore that it was very hard to get men to enlist as carriers.

The initial problems were how to register the carriers and how to pay them. A District Commissioner gave each headman a list of his batch of recruits, and then sent the duplicate copy to the Carrier Depot Officer at Kisumu, Nairobi or Mombasa. The officer commanding one of the thousand-strong "Corps" kept the nominal roll, notifying payments and alterations to carrier headquarters in Nairobi, where they kept duplicate rolls and drew cash from the civil treasury. Very soon, the system was in trouble. Military and civil records differed, and endless confusion ensued as many men deserted to join friends in other units under different names, or died without their deaths being recorded; hence, vanished without trace.

A pay roll of Carrier Corps No.7 shows three headmen and twenty-one men of Company No. 70 from Nyanza Province. Three were repatriated from Kajiado Hospital. A fourth, Orowa Ofwani, was sent to Longido Hospital on 20th December 1914, but he could not be traced although every hospital book along the Namanga line was searched. Let us imagine how this might have happened: Suppose that a Mr.Otieno meets a friend from home called Obondo, who is a servant with a regiment on its way south. Since Otieno wants to be with his friend Obondo, he deserts and, calling himself Onyango, becomes a servant to a European officer whom he follows during the 1916 offensive. If he dies, this sad but not an unlikely event may never be officially known since "Onyango" has no number or place on any roll. In this fictitious case, Otieno was at first a deserter, but unless his survival could be proved, he would finally be a "missing person, presumed dead."

When the carrier section took over control in December 1914, the Depots kept records and paid balances on discharge. In March 1915, the East Africa Pay Corps took over payment of labour units from the civil authorities. Confusion remained as different units competed and took each other's deserters. A unit could still have on roll, men who were unknown to the carrier section or depots. District Commissioners were not blameless either. They supplied labour directly to the military without reference to the carrier section thereby falsifying its statistics and causing men to lose pay, especially if they were issued to officers with no authority to pay them.

The Native Followers Recruitment Ordinance, June 1915, meant compulsion, and the basic wage later went down to Rs. 5 a month for the first three months of service, rising to Rs. 6 thereafter, with higher rates for those with special skills. Trouble still ensued where a man had not previously been registered with the carrier section. Malashi, for example, formerly a military employee, became a sweeper with the 2nd Rhodesia Regiment. "He is now at Voi and can no doubt assist in tracing himself," wrote Watkins to the DC.[20] As Malashi had no number, it may not have been so easy to trace him. On the other hand, who could be sure whether a man who existed only as a name and number on a roll, with perhaps Rs. 49 due to him, was alive, dead, deserted or on another roll under another name?

With all this confusion, grave difficulties were inevitable when men were discharged. Until General Smuts' offensive began in February 1916, carriers served for between six and nine months. Rejects and repatriates would report in batches to their DCs to be paid off. Unless a man had documents to prove his status, it was difficult to pay him off. For example, Bakari bin Salim was jailed at Mombasa because he could not pay Rs. 3 tax. He was on the roll of Carrier Corps No. 1, and said he was owed Rs. 80, but that his discharge certificate had been taken from him by a certain carrier officer. That particular officer's reputation inclined one to believe Bakari. "If this was true, things must be put right," said his D.C., "but if not, I should be glad to be in a position to deny it."[21]

Bakari may probably have deserted which could be the reason he had not been paid off. It was always difficult to substantiate a story of discharge without pay. New instructions were sent to Depot Officers whereby the most reliable man in a batch took the pay voucher to the D.C.'s office, the D.C. having received a duplicate by post. Receipts were thumb-printed and returned to carrier headquarters. Since the men were only rationed to the place where they were paid off, it was up to them to claim their pay at once. If a carrier had been on active service, he might have drawn no pay for some time, and therefore have a reasonable sum to his credit when discharged.

Death registers were kept at each depot, and monthly lists appeared in carrier section orders. A D.C. paid relations and sent claims to the Depot Officer. If a man's death could not be proved, his name was not registered and his relations could not be paid. Early in 1916, there were complaints that lists were not reaching D.C.s, who could then not pay claims. Watkins agreed with H.R. Tate, P.C. Kenia, who presumed that this was due to the growing pressure of military demands. The carrier section was, he said, short-staffed and already responsible for 20,000 men.

Clearly, the carrier staff needed to have more authority. The system had to be more closely organised, and above all there had to be an end to unauthorised labour recruiting. Early in 1916, the Military Labour Bureau was set up to administer all followers, except for those employed by the military railways. Its headquarters was at Race Course Road Camp, the Nairobi Carrier Depot. Watkins was Director of Military Labour, but his junior rank of Lieutenant-Colonel gave him too little authority, considering that he probably commanded more men than all other Deserters units put together. The system which he now built up was based on his former experience in South Africa as a clerk in the Pretoria Town council.

The Assistant Paymaster (carriers) controlled all carrier pay accounts, and even distributed cash to all combatant units. No follower could now be paid without a disc, a depot number and an account. The statistical section recorded all deaths and their causes, all enlistments, discharges and desertions. An identity system was set up, based on the finger print section and *Kipandes* (the numbered metal discs) which were issued to each man. Paper *Kipandes* proved useless, as Captain Carnelly reported in December 1916. A man could draw pay anywhere; then the local paymaster would notify the drawer's Depot which kept his Paycard. He could now be identified and credited with his dues even if he lost his disc. Any Depot could issue a new disc and number. The finger print section could trace his old number, and the Pay Office could transfer his credits to his new number. 10,000 lost disc numbers had been traced and their owners re-registered by February 1919.

Pay cards were not introduced until July 1916. The backlog of work was almost impossible to overcome. So, it was decided that a man's word as to how much he was owed at discharge would have to be accepted. The cost of keeping him until his balance was worked out would be greater than any overpayment. Then came the mass levy, and there were 70,000 unbalanced cards at Nairobi, needing 50 extra clerks to get them straight. The work involved was mind boggling. At the end of 1917, there was a shortage of cash to pay the vast numbers being discharged. The Indian Government was reluctant to provide coin and there was once a riot when notes were offered instead. The East Africa Protectorate still depended on India for currency until the post-war currency reforms.

The war caused a great increase in wage-earning when so many had served as soldiers and followers. Some squandered their money at dukas as happened to a KAR corporal from Meru, Muthanya, who seems to have thought he was going to get more later. Others, like Mbwika Kivandi of Kilungu in Machakos District, were more prudent. He put his askari's pay towards his dowry of goats and beer. Another one is a South Nyanza stretcher bearer, Nguka Nyaoke, who spent Rs. 60 on a big bull. Okech Atonga, a machine-gun carrier, brought his father Rs. 500 to pay tax; while members of the Kikuyu Mission Volunteers at Kahuhia, Murang'a District, bought cows, sheep and goats. Those from the group who were young enough went back to school, and others got married.

According to Muasya Maitha, an ammunition carrier, and Umoa Mbatha, a headman, both of Muthetheni, Machakos District, some carriers spent their pay to supplement their diet, especially snuff, on food in the areas they were fighting in. The Nyala askari, Odandayo Agweli, and Asembo Odera, his neighbour, are other examples of more prudent carriers. Agweli bought many cows and blankets while Odera paid Rs. 500 for three wives whose labour he would need having lost a leg in battle. Odera remarked,

> "Even to this day, I still get some money. I wondered very much what happened to the salaries of my friends who were unlucky enough to die, because their listed relations got nothing".[22]

Muasya and Umoa had this to say:

> "When a death list reached the D.C., an announcement was made, asking the relatives of men who did not come home to go to a baraza. Kyethe's wife went, crying. Umoa had broken the sad news to her, but she

had not believed him. He had died of dysentery. She was given his money."[23]

In April 1915, a KAR Regulation gave followers the same right to compensation as soldiers. The colonial government was ready to pay blood money for having sent a man to his death, but the military refused to compensate the relatives of the dead unless he was a professing Christian or Mohammedan. The War Office and Treasury in London endorsed this distinction between "non-pagans" and "pagans" and were obstinately determined to stop payment by tribal custom. All government officers were aware that the next-of-kin was the eldest surviving male relative in most tribes.

The colonial government could spend its own money without reference to the military. For example, death list No. 8 of January 1916 named eight men killed at Mwele, in Gazi District. The D.C., G.H. Osborne, had personally engaged one, named Kinga Kome, whose balance of Rs. 49.50 was paid to his brother as next-of-kin. A Ganda driver called Nasanairi Mayanja had died in Dar es Salaam on 4th July 1917. His brother, Simeyu Kadu, was paid his balance of Rs. 22.40, but was refused compensation which could only be paid to the widow and child.

The East Africa Protectorate government conferred with the military, and in 1918, Legislative Council passed the *"Military Labour Distribution of Pay and Personal Property Ordinance."* Under Section 18, balances unclaimed in three years were to go to the benefit of the tribes concerned. Incredible though it seems, the failure of the Colonial Office to get the consent of the War Office and Treasury to this just proposal was made an excuse for refusing any settlement of the unclaimed wages which were due to missing carriers. In 1920, Lord Milner, Colonial Secretary, was forced to order the Government of Kenya (as it had now become) to repeal Section 13. A storm of protest ensued, led by Ainsworth and Watkins, who saw it as a breach of faith between himself and the men he had led. There had been no identity system till 1916. Paying claims through District Officers, and crediting unpaid balances to tribal authorities, cost the British Government much less than a special military staff would have done.

In 1921, the Native Trust Fund Ordinance had endorsed the payment of unclaimed balances to the tribes. Despite protests from officials, settlers and missionaries in Kenya, and from the new Colonial Secretary, Winston Churchill, Section 13 was finally repealed in 1922. The sum outstanding for all the East African territories was now about £165,123.75. Payments went on wherever claimants could be found, and subject to military prejudices. In 1924, the new Labour Colonial Secretary vainly put the claim again to the War Office. Kenya was in debt after the war, and the cost could not be met in London. His successor, Leo Amery, blamed the War Officer for the absence of a military transport organisation in the first place, and secondly, for dissenting from the agreement between the military and colonial authorities in East Africa.

The German economy was far weaker than that of Britain, yet they had paid out £300,000 to meet claims in Tanganyika. The attitude of the War Office and Treasury therefore invited a most unfavourable comparison with the German Government. The comparison was a new argument used in Despatch No. 83, which followed consultations between Nairobi and the Colonial Office, and was signed by the acting Governor of Kenya on 7th February 1931.

Despatch No. 83 gives the history of the "porters' claim", summarising every despatch between London and Nairobi since the end of the war, in forceful language and in careful detail. All the arguments used by both sides are set out. It describes the recruiting and registering of carriers, explaining why the early records were imperfect, and why names caused such difficulty. For example, a "false" name might be a commemoration of some feat, while in some tribes, custom forbade a man from giving his true name. Eventually, there was unanimity between the Kenya Government and several Colonial Secretaries against the War Office's decision to refuse to pay against a "false" name. The tribes had never fully recovered from the wartime absence of so many able-bodied men, and from the loss of so many lives. Refusal to pay dues on such flimsy reasons would therefore, be a terrible blow on them. The whole document throbs with a very real sense of the anger felt at the callous rejection of "the porters' claim" by War Office and Treasury officials. Unfortunately, 1931 was a year of economic depression and the claim was again rejected.

The exact position on 31 August 1930 was as follows:

Table 3: Number of Missing Men and the Unpaid Claims

Country	Number of missing men 31.03.22	Unpaid wages 31.08.30	Unpaid wages 31.08.30
Kenya	13,748	10,301	£ 49,234
Tanganyika	27,535	27,422	£ 90.470
Uganda	780	855	£ 3,345
Zanzibar and Mafia	349	645	£ 7,537
Totals	**42,421**	**39,223**	**£ 150,586**

3,447 claims had been met in Kenya but in Tanganyika, only 113 had gone through. By 1922, missing men could safely be presumed dead, except perhaps in Tanganyika where a wartime deserter stood more chances of getting home. However, the statistical confusion in that country was extreme. The high wages which Zanzibar carriers were able to command are reflected in the size of the claim.

In the end, Kenya won an *ex gratia* payment of £ 50,000, due to a recommendation of the Morris Carter Land Commission of 1934 (s2048-s2068). The old, well-known and well justified arguments were employed again. The award was accompanied by a complaint that the Commission had given its views without the other side of the story being heard. Whoever wrote this complaint had presumably not read the history of "the porters' claim", notably Despatch No. 83. Both sides of the dispute had been well publicised since the end of the war. As the award did not apply to Tanganyika, an official at Dar es Salaam refrained with difficulty, from expressing an opinion but there was no need as the facts of this sorry tale speak for themselves.

The Bishop of Northern Rhodesia, Alston May, is said to have been very angry with the government of that protectorate for neglecting its servicemen. A good illustration of the whole saga is Joseph Mwenya's story. He was from Kawambwa near the Luapula River. Mwenya had served as a carrier with the British South Africa Police for nothing. He then became a servant to a South African officer and was badly wounded at the battle of Mahiwa. He worked at Tanga for many years and his leg eventually had to be amputated in the government hospital there. The DC Mufulira (on the Copperbelt) sent a request for information to the Secretariat, Lusaka, which finally reached Dar es Salaam. ,Joseph Mwenya probably got compensation, as the evidence was very clear. He would not, of course, have been on the books of the Military Labour Bureau.[29]

Notes

1. Watkins Papers, R9.
2. Scott to Watkins, 19 Oct. 1914.
3. Watkins Papers, R15, Secretary, Central Committee of Supply to Director, Supply, 27 November, 1914.
4. Ibid., private, 4 December, 1914; R16, 29, Nov. 1914.
5. C.J. Wilson. *The Story of the East African Mounted Rifles* (Nairobi, 1938), 44- quoted Clyde, *Medical Services*, 58-59.
6. Watkins to Pike, 6 Jan. 1918; Watkins Report, paragraphs 63 and 110.
7. Watkins Papers, R18, 9 December 1914, copies to Chief Secretaries, Nairobi and Entebbe, Supply Officer Kilindini, and Ainsworth.
8. Ibid., R111, Watkins to Deputy Adjutant and Quartermaster General, 16 July, 1917.
9. Notes kindly given by Dr. J. Forbes Munro.
10. Hill, *Permant Way*, Vol. II, 157.
11. Watkins papers, Watkins to Deputy Adjutant and Quartermaster-General, 19 April 1917, and letters earlier that month.
12. W.H. Kauntze, "A Polyvalent Vaccine in the Treatment of Bacillary Dysentery in East Africa" Journal of Hygiene 18, 4 (1920).
13. Watkins Report, paragraph 28.
14. Ibid., R53-7, 23 December 1916 to Jan. 1917.
15. Ibid., R58-69, March-April, 1917.
16. Ibid., R73-6, 17-21, April 1917.
17. Captain J.H. Carnelly's Report, 20th Jan., 1917.
18. Watkins papers, Lyon's letters: to Watkins, 11 December, 1917.
19. Military Lbaour Bureau Handbook, paragraph 19.
20. Kenya National Archives, 37/577 2, Watkins to Platts (DC Voi), 23 Aug. 1915.
21. Kenya National Archives, 37/577 2, Dundas (DC) to Watkins, 10 Aug. 1915; for Kerslake Thomas see, *OG*, 1914, 1124; see also 38/582, "Labour

Requirements and Recruiting", and 37/577 5, 767, where his foreman was convicted of assault while recruiting.

22 Interview at Bunyala on 4th July, 1970.
23 Interview at Muthetheni on 14 June, 1969.

Chapter Six

Effects of the War

Experience

Muthii onaga magothe - He who travels sees many things
(Kikuyu proverb)

"Few have written of the devastating effect of the war on the African himself", wrote Dr. Philp, summarising the drastic impact on those who survived.[1] Among the horrors and disasters of war, boredom was the greater enemy. However, there were other experiences, both amusing and instructive. The African learnt that firearms, field guns, ammunition, wireless sets and motor vehicles were not magical, but inanimate objects needing both muscle and brain to make them work. A British soldier, Driver Campbell, described some men pushing a lorry out of the mud: *"Von Lettow, oh! Von Lettow, oh! Von Lettow, kwenda!"*[2] With a mighty heave and a marked sense of humour, they completed a routine task.

War is enlightening; it is also a great leveller. Campbell and eleven other white drivers, wilting in the heat of the Ruvuma valley, were forced by a bullying European NCO to help Africans to unload stores. Finally, they escaped and left it to the Africans, who no doubt noticed yet again that they could stand the heat better than Europeans. Sir Philip Mitchell, a District Officer in Nyasaland who served in the KAR and was later appointed the Governor of Kenya, noted that the white man lost prestige when askaris learned that they too could kill

Germans. Further more, everyone slept on the ground when in the field, and Africans could watch Europeans dressing, undressing, washing and shaving.

Charles Hobley shows that there were many ways in which Africans could see themselves as equal or superior to Europeans:

> "They saw Europeans shot down and even bayonetted by enemy black soldiers, they realised that very few Europeans were crack shots, they noted the inferior marching capacity of the white man, his inability to find his way about the bush without a native guide, and in some cases they even saw that the courage of the white man was not greater than that of the black."[3]

This equality or superiority to Europeans was shown when Mtole, a post near Kilwa, was attacked, and a carrier captain and other whites narrowly escaped court-martial for cowardice. If a European needed to have "jiggers" removed from his feet, it could best be removed safely, though painfully, by an African with the necessary skill, as Dr. Dolbey testified. This common pest, incidentally, caused many casualties, and prevented men from marching.

Dr. Brett Young gives a drastic illustration of the levelling effects of war with his story of how he spent a night in the bush with Nyanza stretcher bearers and wounded Indians, hiding from the Germans who had rushed their clearing station. He was greatly impressed by the cheerfulness shown by the Nyanza men "under the most distressing physical conditions," and of the resourcefulness shown by one who kept a dry mealie cob glowing all night, from which they lit their tobacco on the march.

Reri's story in *Red Strangers* is one of unrelieved horror. The train journey and sea voyage were terrifying, especially when a fear-maddened man threw himself overboard. This ship sounds less disgusting than the lake steamers, or the Wang Hai I (known as the One Lung). In April 1917, 13 porters had died on board this ship and 100 more after disembarking at Mombasa. Probably there was some failure of supervision. None of the men interviewed had any complaint to make about ships. There were never enough ships, and the Military Labour Bureau was lucky to have had two wheezy transports in succession, as well as its own hospital ship.

Contact with West Africans gave East Africans much to think about. The Europeans discouraged fraternisation, spreading false rumours about cannibalism. Kinuthia, who was attached to the KMV, said that at Dodoma, they met Makorogothi [Gold Coasters], who were said to be cannibals. The Kikuyu made friends and traded with them. Kinuthia also said that they had their wives with them, but he might have been mistaken because the Gold Coast Regiment were in fact on the Kilwa line and had no women with them. Besides, the KMV were supporting the Belgian advance on Mahenge, so presumably, these men were Congolese. Nevertheless, the subject of cannibalism was so sensitive that a Force Order threatened British officers and other ranks with disciplinary action if they spread such rumours. But the Belgian force were so poorly disciplined that there is little doubt that some of the men were cannibals. For instance, the KAR historian notes an instance where a cannibal meal was said to have been cooked on a railway platform.

Musembi Kiindu, an ammunition carrier whom we met in the Kilungu Hills, said that he and his friends had actually caught some cannibals in the act; the carrier officer had kicked the *nyama* into the bush, and the Kamba had to protect him. Musembi said that they were Nigerian soldiers, but the Nigerians and their front-line carriers were mostly Muslims and Hausa, so they can be ruled out. Josphat Njoroge, KMV had heard that Belgian soldiers were cannibals; he said that they were called "Bolomatari" (breakers of obstacles), a nickname of H.M. Stanley, the explorer.

Carriers kept on the whole to their own ethnic groups, according to Jonathan Okwirri, who was a superior headman for two years at the Mombasa Depot. There may have been periodic brawls but war can also break down barriers as Mwika Kivandi, KAR, from Kilungu observed. He said that they would make friends with their comrades, as one would expect of soldiers. Kinyanjui wa Mukura supported him and said: "If you became ill, whatever tribe you came from, I would look after you and cook for you."[4] Many carriers learned Swahili, and with it a wider knowledge of the world.

What did servicemen talk about and do in their spare time? Some of them felt that discussing homely things like ceremonies and customs might only increase their homesickness. Others liked to sing songs to do with the war, like this one quoted by Mutiso Kanzivei (Machakos) about a one-eyed corporal who was cruel to the askari:[5]

Musikali wi Nthongo	*Soldier blind in one eye*
Nthongo isu	*That blind eye*
Yootwika to-kongo furrow	*Might become like a*
Kana ukalika ndutu	*Or get a flea in it*
Ukanyeewa!	*And itch!*

Another song was quoted by Mbwika Kivandi in which the Nzama (Council) are accused of hoping that askaris would die:

> *That I will not do, Council*   *To enjoy the company*
> *But will go back home*   *Of beautiful women!"*

No doubt girls and hopes of marriage, if and when they returned home, were frequently discussed. The two Nyala askaris, Agweli and Odera, talked a lot about women, their homes and customs.

Jonathan Okwirri had much to say about spare-time activities in Mombasa Depot where men kept themselves happy after working hours with singing, dancing, playing football and discussing. They could get special leave to go into Mombasa within a time limit and within a four mile radius. They talked about themselves and the different types of people whom they met: Europeans, Arabs, Zanzibaris, other kinds of Africans, and even Chinese (probably members of a stevedore company whom they called "twins" because they were so alike). They discussed the sickness and suffering so evident in the broken men who returned by sea for treatment in the hospital and convalescent camp.

A lot has already been said about discipline and control, which are two sides of the same coin. The East African Force as a whole suffered permanently from bad discipline. Watkins was expected to run the Military Labour Bureau, with as many men as all the rest put together. Though only a Lieutenant-Colonel; his request to be a full Colonel was turned down by his chief, Brig. ᵈier-General Fendall, with whom his relations were never easy. C ⋯ ᵗt for Watkins' authority as Director of Military Labour, anc.   ᵗᵉ regulations, greatly increased the suffering of carriers.

Various Force Orders forbade commanding officers to march troops unnecessarily in the heat of the day. They were also supposed to observe health precautions and water discipline. which is expressly mentioned in *Paragraph 19* of the *Military Labour Bureau Handbook,* already cited as the basis for carrier management. *Paragraph 19* covers every aspect of labour management so thoroughly that after the war, Watkins, as Chief Native Commissioner, re-issued it in the Official Gazette. Officers who were accessible to their men. and treated them fairly and justly, would always be backed up in tight places; "an officer with no direct control will be deserted at the first excuse".[6]

For discipline, carriers were subject to the 1912 KAR Ordinance. A commanding officer could order up to 24 lashes. 42 days imprisonment with or without hard labour. and 21 days loss of pay. A detachment commander could order 14 days imprisonment and 10 days loss of pay. Lashes were given with the buttocks covered by wet cloth, 12 hours after sentence and under medical supervision. Major Lyon breached these orders in more ways than one. More brutal methods in 1903 so disgusted Meinertzhagen that he refused to allow a man of his to be flogged again, unless he was then discharged. A Meru askari. M'Laibuni wa Baikwamba, exhibited his scars uninvited to his interviewer; while Marius Karatu said he was caned for desertion at Moshi.

Captain Maxted, Post Commandant at Kisumu. and not a Carrier Officer, gave two carrier headmen 84 days hard labour each (for theft and assault). Major E.L. Scott tried to protect Maxted against the consequences of exceeding his powers so grossly by asking for a private explanation: why had a carrier officer not dealt with the case, and could he send a copy of his instructions? Maxted told his senior officer from the Line of Communications, Dar es Salaam: "I will not be dictated to by you."[7] This officer, who was clearly on good terms with Watkins, gave Maxted some sort of reprimand. The fact that a mere captain, guilty of a grave breach of discipline, felt free to treat a lieutenant-colonel, the head of an important department, with such contempt and defiance shows again how impossible it was to protect the interests of carriers. In his report, Watkins called his officers "fearless champions" of their men, meaning that their rights were continually in jeopardy.

Mumbi Mulei, a Kamba medical orderly, mentioned running a man about with a load of salt as a punishment. Others remembered marching with a rifle for several hours. Jonathan Okwirri mentioned that a load of 60 lbs might sometimes be given, instead of the standard 50 lbs, though in fact most men carried 60 lbs, when extras like tools, cooking pots or personal odds and ends were included.

M'Inoti, Meru postal carrier, voiced the general opinion that while some officers were harsh, most were considerate. He spoke of a very brave captain called *Mwanoiba* who was killed in action. Nduma Mutie, carrier headman, mentioned two very considerate officers who were well-known farmers at Kiu: *Kitila* (Major Frank Joyce) and *Kiteng'e* (Captain Wilson). Some of the best NCOs in the KAR were the Sudanese or Nubians whose descendants live at Bondo near Kampala, and at Kibera in Nairobi. Odandayo Agweli, KAR, said what tough disciplinarians the two Nubians in his company were. He recalled an incident showing that askaris were not disposed to take harsh treatment lying down. During a food strike, Sergeant

Sefi, an Arab, knocked down Agweli's friend Ouma. In retaliation, Agweli knocked Sefi down. As a punishment, Agweli was given several hours extra drill by a white officer nicknamed *Bwana Mukia* because of his fly-whisk.

There were two instances of really cruel officers or NCOs being killed by their own men. Mbwika Kivandi, KAR, said that a white NCO used to beat the men to wake them up. So one day at 6.30 a.m. they beat him to death. They stood silently in three concentric circles till noon. When the colonel came, he only said *"Ni shauri ya vita tu"* (it is an act of war), in order to avert a mutiny. Okech Atonga who was a gun carrier with 4th KAR, said that an officer called *Kibaya* (Bad man) was killed by his men after ill-treating them for a year.

The rapid growth of the KAR and Carrier Corps brought in many white men who were new to Africa; some of whom were described by one of the Official Historian's correspondents as a "a poor, shell-shocked lot". A sergeant-major of 2nd KAR asked "Of what tribe do these new masters come?" Certainly, some were steeped in white South African prejudices. With the enormous difficulties in staffing, it is a wonder that the new forces did so well.[8]

When conscripted for military service, most men, will adapt fairly quickly, and develop a professional pride and *esprit de corps*. The more enterprising will always try to improve their status, and to put their strength and courage to the test in order to gain promotion. In the Carrier Corps, promotion meant better pay and clothing as visible signs of higher status. An ordinary carrier was paid Rs.6 a month, and was given only a jumper, a blanket and a haversack, but a stretcher bearer, gun carrier or signal porter also got shoes, putties, shorts, a tarboosh, and

Rs.15. Syces, veterinary dressers, armed scouts, interpreters and telegraph workers also did better than the rank-and-file. The carrier police were, as expected, the best dressed of all. Though their pay is not recorded, they could hardly have had less than armed scouts, who got Rs.20. They were raised originally to prevent desertions on the Mikesse-Rufiji line, were armed and relieved troops of many guard duties. As a superior headman, Jonathan Okwirri was paid Rs.12, and had a woollen shirt called a *magari* as a mark of status. As a rule, first-line carriers had to be of superior physique, and as well trained and disciplined as soldiers. They went to special depots like Kwa Maleve near Ngong. When the first recruits saw their uniforms and heard that they were to be drilled like askaris, they were delighted.

Team work had to be instilled. The problems of getting a Vickers heavy machine gun into action was described earlier where it was explained that each gun was served by two soldiers, fourteen carriers, a donkey- boy and five donkeys. It consisted of a barrel and tripod (each weighing 60 Ibs), with other spare parts and ammunition in boxes weighing 60 Ibs each. In 1914, a battalion of 800 men had only two such guns, so that a large part of its firepower was lost if an enemy ambush caused porters to drop their loads and flee. Laden porters could not take cover as fast as soldiers. Similar problems arose when carrying Lewis light machine-guns, stokes mortars and their bombs, and above all parts of 2.95" mountain guns. In Captain Downes' book, there is a picture of a Nigerian battery carrier, with the wheel of a gun on his head, its iron tyre across his shoulder, totalling 70 Ibs.

First-line carriers were also soldiers in the real sense. At the battle of Mahiwa, a Nigerian gun carrier won the Military Medal (MM) for fighting with a rifle. Another won the

Distinguished Conduct Medal (DCM: a higher award) for bringing up shells for a mountain gun; joining its crew as the gunners fell and then using a rifle against the oncoming foe. The DCM was awarded to a stretcher bearer for disregarding his personal safety under fire, so as to be ready with his stretcher.

Most regrettably, awards for bravery were not issued to East African carriers, although there is ample evidence that they behaved with equal courage. Captain Thomas Anderson said of the work of porters and personal servants: "The regularity with which these men ran the gauntlet of rifle, machine-gun and shell fire, bringing up food and ammunition to the various outposts is worthy of all praise".[9] Fortunately, War Memorials were set up in 1927 in Nairobi, Mombasa and Dar es Salaam. Tributes were also published in the *Mombasa Times* to the KAR, Arab Rifles, Intelligence Scouts and Carrier Corps. Instances were given of bravery as great as that of Lance-Corporal Sowera of 2/2nd (Nyasa) KAR, who won the DCM for firing his Lewis gun all day from a tree, and then dancing *ngoma* to hearten his men. A Nyanza ammunition carrier who continued to bear his load to the firing line after one hand had been shattered by a bullet was also commended. A porter was rewarded for taking a soldier's place in the line at the defence of Jasin. One sympathises with gun carriers who replaced the patches of yellow cloth in their tarbooshes with KAR cap badges, a practice which had been forbidden. Nevertheless, some first-line carriers like Kimumo Kitui, a stretcher bearer, were transferred to the KAR because of their military prowess.

The carriers who were killed in action were mostly front-line men, who shared the dangers faced by soldiers. Sometimes, a man sought death as a welcome relief from the horrors around him., like Reri in *Red Strangers*. Musembi Kiindu said that he once stood up in the hope that he might be killed but was forced by an officer to lie down. William , KAR, of South Nyanza said that he smeared himself with a comrade's blood and pretended to be dead. This showed both courage and presence of mind. His neighbour, Lazaro Maende, lost a finger while carrying ammunition. Ngugi, a Kiambu gun carrier, was shot through the arm by a bullet which also scraped his upper lip. He spoke highly of the kindness of European nurses, and of the cleanliness of the hospital ship. Undoubtedly, many others bore honourable scars to the grave, as tokens of their devotion to duty.

An unauthorised practice which was employed more than once on the Kagera front, west of Lake Victoria, was to use carriers as decoys to distract the enemy's attention. One instance was at Bukoba before the raid in 1915, when 1,000 porters simulated troops in full view of the enemy. Had the Germans then shelled them, the casualties would have been severe.

Let us end on a lighter note. One of the *wazee* at Ngecha (Kiambu District) said that at Mwanza there were some trees, whose smell caused madness. Had he been there himself, or did he hear this from someone else? No more can be said of this traveller's tale!

Post War Political Developments in Africa

I think things happened the way they did because the world was still asleep. We Africans were still powerless and had to fight for the strong man, whom we believed was fighting for wealth.
(Nguka Nyaoke, stretcher bearer)

Historians have been trying to find out to what extent wartime experience affected post-war political developments in Africa. This book can only consider how the war affected the East

Africa Protectorate, which became the Crown Colony of Kenya in July 1920. Before the war, the impact of colonial government on African society had been limited to those districts most affected by labour recruiting, where land had been taken by the Europeans or was felt to be under threat. Also, where the missions had developed education. These areas were Kiambu, Murang'a and Central Nyanza. The young men who were literate in Swahili and English, and were already making their way in the world in 1914, included those prominent in the political protest movements of the 1920s.

In 1928, a senior official, R.W. Hemsted, wrote that the war had taught Africans the power of organisation which was in some way connected with the protest movements. In what way? The answer is best sought by seeing what these young leaders were doing during the war. Josiah Njonjo, Koinange wa Mbiu, Philip Karanja, and Waruhiu wa Kungu are four prominent examples. They became senior chiefs in Kiambu. Njonjo was a compositor on *The Leader,* then clerk to the DC Ngong, with whom he went on safaris to the German border. Of the others, only Karanja was on war service as a superior headman with the Kikuyu Mission Volunteers.

For the opposition, Harry Thuku was a compositor and machine man with, *The Leader,* which would not let him go and fight. He alone knew how to print maps and sketches of war positions. Jomo Kenyatta was in the Public Works Department. Joseph Kang'ethe, who was for 20 years president of the Kikuyu Central Association, was a gun carrier headman. A Murang'a man, James Beauttah, was a telephonist and not allowed to join the KAR.

Jonathan Okwirri's experience as a superior headman offered

him a valuable training for post-war leadership in Central Nyanza. He spent eighteen months at Mombasa Depot where he had better access to the news than most members of the Carrier Corps. After the war, he became a senior chief and president of the Young Kavirondo Association. Despite the alarm caused in Uyoma in 1912 by the land alienations in Nandi and the European's bad treatment of labour, Okwirri said that they had not thought of the European as a bad man. However, he added:

> "When the word began to go around that Kenya was to become a colony, those of us who had some understanding, at least could read and write, [knew that] a colony means a settlement containing foreigners, [and that] finally the land would fall into the foreigners' hands."[10]

Though politics was not discussed at the depot, Okwirri read *The Standard, The Leader, The Juati Luo* and various Swahili papers, and foresaw that a Crown Colony could become a Dominion. His words:

> "Even if the settlers held land in the Rift Valley, and we people in Uyoma still had our land, the land would not be held in our name; it would be in the name of the Dominion. We didn't have anything particularly in mind, except that all we eventually wanted was that our country should remain our country."[11]

Apart from Okwirri and Kang'ethe, most leaders with war experience seem to have been in the KMV, serving for only 10 months in a carefully run unit with far better conditions than most. A minor activist in the Limuru area was Marius Karatu, with his varied service as ox-cart driver and medical dresser. He said that looking after the sick left little time to talk politics: "We were not politicians then; what was worrying us was the war." He was, however, given some sound advice by Indians:

> "When the war is over, Mzungu will take your land. What you will be given afterwards will be identity cards. You will also be mistreated, and some will be detained and taken into exile in some far islands, as it was done to Napoleon and Gandhi."[12]

Men with enough education to be clerks either worked at home, like Raphael Osodo who was chief's clerk in Bunyala, or Elijah Kaara, who was first a clerk at the Nairobi Carrier Depot, and then a storeman in German East Africa. Nairobi was a better school for a future politician than Dodoma, Lindi, the Rufiji or even Dar es Salaam. Most of the men we have been discussing spent the war in or near Nairobi. Harry Thuku says what they talked about in his Autobiography:

> "I read many of the articles that the settlers wrote to *The Leader* (the paper was strongly in favour of the white settlers), and when I saw something there about the treatment of Africans, it entered into my head and lay quiet there until later on."[13]

He had frequent discussions with Koinange wa Mbiu: "I saw he was quite fearless. He was very much opposed to what had happened to Kikuyu land."[14] A neighbour of Marius Karatu, Joseph Mundia, was conscripted in 1915, fell ill at Voi and worked as a cook, his pre-war vocation, first in Indian messes and then for junior officers near Kilimanjaro. He said that when he came back, his brother was forced to go to the war instead of him. The brother never came back.

Mundia was most definite that the first political leaders were those who stayed at home. His spontaneous and incidental rejection of any direct link between the war and the political leadership is evident:

> "They could see how we were being treated. People did not start politics because of what they were being told by those who came back from the war, but because of the things which were happening here; girls were being forced to work, and if your sheep or goat was found by the roadside, it would be taken." (Presumably by the tribal police).[15]

Though his war service was much less than that of others, Mundia typifies thousands of men who were very concerned with developments at home. Karatu agreed with this. So did Nathaniel Mahingu and Kinyanjui wa Mukura, who were emphatic that they started politics because of their land.

We have seen how the war increased settler power through the Committees of Supply, the War Council, and various Ordinances and Commissions. The Native Registration Ordinance of 1916 introduced the *kipande* or the identity token, which was enacted in 1919, and became a major grievance. Ironically, it was vital to the running of the Carrier Corps, particularly in ensuring that men got their pay. Crown Colony status, which worried Okwirri and his friends, was advocated by *The Leader,* and was an objective of the Land Settlement and Economic Commissions of 1917, with their settler majorities.

Settler ambitions were well known to all Africans who could read, and to many who could not. Servants, for instance, might have known enough English to understand political discussions at European dinner tables. This is hinted at by G.A.S.

Kinyanjui wa Mukura and Nathaniel Mahingu

Northcote, DC Kiambu, who says that everyone was discussing the Land Settlement Commission recommendations about using land from the reserves for Soldier Settlements. Ewart Grogan trumpeted all the settler views in his notorious speech in February 1919 at the dinner of welcome to the new Governor, General Sir Edward Northey. The Governor was told in effect that he was only welcome if he supported the settlers.

All this led to consultations, involving on the one hand, chiefs led by Kinyanjui wa Gatherimu and Koinange wa Mbiu, and on the other, Harry Thuku and his friends. Their joint memorandum was translated by A.R. Barlow, who had served as an officer in the Kikuyu Mission Volunteers. A *baraza* was held at Dagoretti on 24th June 1921, a memorable day in Kenya political history. Their memorandum submitted five grievances respectfully: One, that Europeans were given land, while African servicemen had no gratuity. (It was wrongly believed that, as well as balances of pay, gratuities would be paid at discharge). Two, the hated *kipande* system, which they wanted abolished Three, that the hut tax had been doubled from Rs.5 to Rs.10, as had the poll tax. Four, that in 1920, the shilling had replaced the rupee, whose value had risen from 1s. 4d. to 2s., but traders tried to give Africans only one shilling for a rupee. Five, that wages had been cut by a third.

They said in the memorandum:

> "When we went to do war work, we were told by His Excellency the Governor that we would be rewarded. But is our reward to have our tax raised, to have registration papers given us and for our ownership of land to be called into question; to be told today that

we are to receive title deeds and tomorrow for it to appear that we are not to receive them?"[16]

The KMV veterans at Kahuhia agreed with the above sentiments and said that political activities in their district were caused by the question of land alienation, and of the awful *kipande* which they considered the "reward" for their services. They also said that land discontent started in Kiambu and then spread to the rest of Kikuyuland. The Dagoretti *baraza* was followed by events that were to later change the history of Kenyan: Harry Thuku took the revolutionary decision to send the memorandum to Britain. Then his arrest and deportation led to a protest meeting and the shooting at the police lines opposite the Norfolk Hotel, Nairobi. After this, his followers started the Kikuyu Central Association. "Even to this day, we belong to KCA," said Nathaniel Mahingu. "Know this, things were started by Harry Thuku," he continued. In Nyeri, Elijah Kaara became a KCA organiser, and showed us a sheaf of papers which concerned arrangements to send Jomo Kenyatta to England. He summed it up as follows: "The Europeans got land; all we got was the *kipande*. "[17]

In Central Nyanza, grievances were similar, but as there was no threat to the land, the Young Kavirondo Association, which was founded by Jonathan Okwirri and his friends, was less militant than Thuku's Young Kikuyu Association. Both got their inspiration from the Young Buganda Association and the Ganda newspaper, *Sekanyolya*, published in Kenya. Its editor, Daudi Basudde, was the telegraphist at Maseno before James Beauttah.

The Young Kavirondo Association (YKA), presented the Governor General, Northey, with a memorandum similar to the

Dagoretti one. They too wanted title deeds, higher wages and the restoration of Protectorate status. It turned into the Kavirondo Taxpayers' Association (KTA) guided by Archdeacon Owen. Jonathan Okwirri explained that *Piny Owacho,* thought by some to be an alternative name to KTA, was in fact a political slogan meaning "The people have said". They were agitating for change. *Piny Owacho* was therefore, a sort of protection so that no single person could be made a scapegoat.

The only link between these protests and the war is that the Dagoretti memorandum draws a comparison between the treatment given to African and European servicemen. In areas where land was not seen to be in danger, the only thought in the minds of returning servicemen was to get back to normal life as soon as possible. Throughout most of Nyanza, this was hindered by famine and disease. Influenza was universal. Diarrhoea and dysentery were brought home by repatriates. This was called *indira* in Nyala, according to Asembo Odera. In Ukambani, it was probably the *isuku* mentioned by Muumbi Mulei. *Bleki* (plague) Plague was reported in Nyala. It was endemic in the Lake region where the Provincial Medical Officer for Nyanza recorded its occurrence annually.

The war was followed by famine called *Keya* (KAR) in Nyala. In North Nyanza, where *mtama* was still the staple food, the famine was *Obando*, the word for maize in South Nyanza, which was able to help out with its surplus. In South Nyanza, the famine was remembered as *kanga*, referring to the maroon jerseys worn by the Askari *Kanga,* the new tribal police.

Throughout the country, men were very reluctant to go out for work with so much to be done at home after years of neglect.

Nguka Nyaoke may have spoken for all when he said:

> "Conditions forced me to stay at home, and not to go to work for a European farmer or any other employer. My elder brother, who had remained at home, had died, so only my father was in the house. I had to remain at home to keep him company. Later, however, I became an askari of my chief".[18]

Okech Atonga also stayed at home, though he worked for a year on the railway extension to Uganda. Otochi Onduko settled at home and tried to forget the war-thirty of his friends had died.

The pattern was just the same in Machakos District. Of the men interviewed, only Nzioki Wambua, KAR, went out to work as a policeman. Another soldier, Kavai Longe, said:

> "I became a teacher, and I taught for 20 years. I also had my business here. I did not work for any European apart from the Catholic missionary who employed me as a teacher. *There were no political meetings, as far as I know, until around the 1950s".* [Author's italics][19]

Thankfully, they reverted to farming. Nguku Mulwa remarked that there were no more raids from the Maasai; that they had been beaten once and for all. Perhaps this was more significant to him than the Europeans' horrible war.

There was little prospect of labour from Ukambani. The DC Kitui, H.R. Montgomery, a brother of the Field-Marshal, said that repatriated carriers were reluctant to go out to work again after their wartime experiences; that they had gone because they had to, and the fact that they had given no trouble could be placed to their credit. Now they were opposed to working on the railway, and from their point of view, he could quite understand it. He was sympathetic, but like some of his colleagues and even some missionaries, he reluctantly concluded that some compulsory labour was inevitable after the war. These were: Ainsworth, Arthur and the Bishops who unwillingly signed Northey's Native Labour Circular No.1. while Frank Weston, Bishop of Zanzibar, indignantly condemned compulsory labour under any circumstances.

Most of the Kamba ex-servicemen donned blankets again. Nguku was wearing one when we met him. Others wore military shorts, which were frowned on by District Officers. One of the District Officers observed:

> "The return of khaki-clad carriers opened the door to the gravest malpractices; tribal retainers used army clothing as their sole badge of office. Returned carriers and KAR showed little respect for elders, and their attitude to Europeans often left much to be desired."[20]

The Provincial Commissioner, Kenia, H.R. Tait, noted similar attitudes.

In his post-war annual report for Kiambu, Northcote shrewdly gave as the root cause of insubordination the fact that their wartime experiences had woken Africans up. The former system of control by both District Officers and headmen had been based on bluff, which had now broken down because the Africans had seen through it and called it off.

Administrative officers praised the people for their acceptance of recruiting. In Ukambani, the PC hoped that the loyalty shown by the native population at a time of exceptional difficulty would long be remembered in its favour. In Nyanza, the PC also commended the fact that in 1920, 38,700 went out to work, although the province had suffered so much from heavy mortality in the war, especially from famine and influenza. Officers also resented settler accusations that they were indifferent to demands for labour, which had already strained relations between chiefs and people before the war. Demands for carriers were fulfilled at an even greater cost in harmony. That was why the government rewarded headmen like Kinyanjui, Mumia and Wambugu with medals.

Africans certainly resented being removed from their homes to participate in a ghastly war which did not seem to concern them as evidenced by some remarks from those among them that survived. Said Odandayo Agweli, KAR: "This was not a fair war because we fought without a cause and, worse still, we lost more men than the whites in our army."[21] His friend, Asembo Odera said:

> "The chiefs should have refused to recruit. It would have been better to let the white men fight themselves without the Africans because we were innocent. And what is more, the white man refused to let us have tribal wars".[22]

However, the main post-war concern in Bunyala, according to Raphael Osodo, was getting rid of the Wanga chief, Kadimu. This was finally accomplished in 1927.

Odera was overlooking the fact that the Europeans could not have fought the war without African assistance. "In this war, the black man is keeping up the courage of the white," wrote Dr. Dolbey in 1918.[23] The sense of obligation which Europeans felt towards Africans for their bravery and endurance was genuine, and there is reason to think that it contributed to better relations and greater tolerance. Settlers thought that it was unjust of the Treasury and War Office not to pay the unclaimed balances of wages, but they themselves still demanded compulsory labour, lower pay and the opening of the reserves for settlement.

African sufferings in the war made it clear that welfare issues which missionaries and officials had been raising to the government before the war, had to be improved. In 1917, Ainsworth, Watkins and Dr. Philp were appalled at the rejection rate in the mass levy. As Chief Native Commissioner, Watkins applied his experience when he reissued *Paragraph 19* of the *Military Labour Bureau Handbook* in the official Gazette as "Instructions for the Care of Labour by Government Departments" but improvement was still much too slow. During the building of the Nyeri and Uasin Gishu railway extensions, the death rate was 8.3%, which would have been thought excessive in wartime. These and similar dietary and medical problems were discussed in the Kenya Medical Journal, started in 1924, by various experts including Dr. C.J. Wilson and Oscar Watkins. Wilson's remarks about rations in Rhodesian mines showed how far behind East Africa was.

Major-General G.J. Giffard, Inspector-General of both the KAR and West African Frontier Force, accepted the Watkins Report and the MLB Handbook as the blueprint for any future military labour organisation. So in 1939, the administrative methods used by the Carrier Corps formed the basis for a new Military Labour Corps and a Pioneer Corps known in Bunyala as *Panyako*. The men had the same pay and rations as white troops. James Beauttah encouraged men to join and there was no compulsion. Chief Josiah Njonjo, from Kenya, and other chiefs from Tanganyika and Uganda went with Mr. S.H. Fazan to inspect African forces in the Middle East and were very satisfied with what they saw. There, men could remit wages home, and there was a good forces mail system. However, the colour bar at home made an ugly contrast to the racial equality experienced in the war. In addition, the new generation of ex-servicemen was more educated than their fathers, and understandably, more discontented.

The missions had provided medical and educational services as a practical demonstration of Christianity. Arthur had hoped that the KMV experience would be an opportunity for evangelism while Dr.Clive Irvine thought that the period after the war had been a time of great spiritual growth. Whilst agreeing with this, Chief Njonjo thought that the movement towards the churches was partly the result of disillusionment with government, the effect of the conscription and suffering of the carriers.

A celebrated Kenyan institution, the Alliance High School, which may be called an indirect memorial to the Carrier Corps came about in this way. After Thuku's arrest in 1922, the KCA began to oppose the education work of the Alliance of Protestant Missions which then began to think of improved schooling as a means of training future leaders. After the Devonshire Declaration of 1923 had ruled that African interests were paramount in Kenya, the settlers advocated technical education. There was, however, an unspent balance of £5,600 from the East African War Relief Fund. The Alliance used this to found a medical college at Kikuyu. A grant of £10,000 by a Nairobi businessman resulted in its completion in 1926 as the Alliance High School, one of the most famous schools in English-speaking Africa.

During the Second World War, Mr. Jack Best, a Kenyan farmer, spoke Swahili from habit in a West African market and was understood by a man who had served in the Nigerian Brigade as a carrier. One can only conclude that it is a small world and Wars have a way of making it even smaller.

Notes

1. H.R.A. Philp, *A New Day in Kenya* (London, 1936), 32.
2. Campbell, *Motor Lorry*, 185.
3. C.W. Hobley, *Bantu Beliefs and Magic* (London: Witherby, 2d. Ed., 1938), 287.
4. Interview at Kabete/Dagoretti.
5. Translation by Courtesy of Augustine Kavyu and David Sperling.
6. Official Gazette, 1921, 184-186.
7. Watkins Papers, Correspondence Oct.-Nov. 1917.
8. Moyse-Bartlett, *KAR* 332-336; Watkins Papers, staff Correspondence; Public Records Office (London), Cabinet Office Papers 45/3/C, Chapter 2, Craftonto Hordern, n.d.
9. Public Record Office (London), Cabinet Office Papers 45/30, to Colonial Secretary, Nairobi, 11 March 1938.
10. Interview, 5 July 1970, assisted by Aloysius Ongutu, his grandson.
11. Ibid.
12. Interviews near Limuru, June and November 1969.
13. Thuku, *Autobiography*, 14-16.
14. Ibid.
15. Interview near Limuru, October 1969.
16. Ross, *Kenya*, 224-227; Thuku, *Autobiography*, 18-22; Rosberg and Nottingham, *Mau Mau*, 36-44.
17. Interview with Mahingu and Mukura, June 1969.
18. Interview at Ithamboni, Machakos, 3 Oct. 1970 (Kathuli).
19. Ibid.
20. Kenya National Archives, DC/MKS/1/1/10, Machakos AR 1918-1919.
21 & 22. Notes kindly given by Felix Osodo; Ertiman Gendia and David Sperling kindly helped with the translation.
23. R.V. Dolbey, *Sketches of the East Africa Campaign* (London, 1918), 118-119; he was Medical Officer with a combatant unit.

Appendix 1

Carrier Corps Recruitment Statistics

1. The East Africa Protectorate

These figures come from provincial and district reports, the latter being preferred where differences arise. In Ukamba, for instance, district reports omit rejects and deserters, who are included in provincial totals. Where figures are lacking, it has usually been possible to calculate (c) from the data given. In Nyanza, the provincial total of 21,925 for the Carrier Corps in 1914-15 seems too high, when only 6,000 worked for the military within the province, and another 4,000 went to Turkana. In Machakos, figures in district reports are preferred to those in political records for 1914-1920 used by Savage and Munro, *Journal of African History*, VII, 2 (1966), pp. 323 and 338.

NYANZA						
Year	Central	North	South	Lumbwa	Nandi	TOTALS
1914-15	4,572	4,372	8,917	78	230	18,169
1915-16	8,888	7,459	6,822	719	296	24,184
1916-17	5,604	6,469	9,558	269	-	21,900
1917-18	8,922	10,036	8,758	68	-	27,784
Totals	27,986	28,336	34,055	1,134	526	92,037

KENIA					
Year	Nyeri	Murang'a	Meru	Embu	TOTALS
1914-15	1,868c	296c	500	2,023c	4,687c
1915-16	2,774	2,021	2,904	2,5442c	10,241c
1916-17	3,671	2,296	216	2,535c	8,718c
1917-18	5,980	4,098	3,854	5,304	19,236
Totals	14,293c	8,711c	7,474	12,404c	42,882c

UKAMBA					
Year	Machakos	Kitui	Kiambu	Nairobi	TOTALS
1914-15	516	(omitted by PC 1917-18)			516
1915-16	2,117	3,064	2,599	747	8,527
1916-17	3,900	3,885	2,359	832	10,976
1917-18	5,076	3,470	2,552	1,345	12,443
Totals	11,609	10,409	7,510	2,924	32,462
Rejects (DC)	-1,120	-2,436	included	(by PC)	-3,556
Final Totals	10,489	7,983	7,510	2,924	28,906

SEYDIE						
Year	Mombasa	Taita	Vanga	Malindi	Nyika	TOTALS
1914-15	?	300	-	280	667c	1,247c
1915-16	952	exempt	264	639	433c	2,288c
1916-17	1,763	exempt	482	62c	1,163	3,470c
1917-18	2,175	2,648	473	251c	2,256	7,803c
Totals	4,890	2,948	1,219	1,232c	4,519	14,808c
Grand Total						178,633c

Appendix

The Military Labour Corps total was 162,578; maybe the difference of 16,055 were rejected at the depots.

2. The Uganda Protectorate

The provincial and district records seem to be more detailed in Kenya than in any other territory. For Uganda, a Secretariat Minute Paper - from Assistant Director of Transport Entebbe, to Chief Secretary Entebbe, H.R. Walli, dated 12/3/17, (National Archives of Uganda, SMP 4290) - gives us a fairly complete picture. This is mostly confirmed by figures supplied by Wallis to Charles Lucas for *The Empire at War* (Oxford 1924). Vol. 4 p. 238, which do not, however, agree with the Military Labour Corps records.

(a) Carriers for military operations in Uganda Aug. - Dec. 1914

MASAKA	KAMPALA TOTALS	ANKOLE	TORO	MUBENDI	
3,000	2,000	1,000	1,000	500	7,500

(b) Uganda Transport Corps Carrier Section

KAMPALA	MUBENDI TOTALS	ANKOLE	JINJA	MASAKA	HOIMA	
5,290	5,019	4,739	4,435	3,119	2,798	25,400
MASINDI	MBALE EP TOTALS	TORO	LANGO EP	TESO EP		
2,272	2,187	1,977	531	529		7,496

(c)

"Special Details": Medical, Gun Porters, Headmen, Ox Transport, Syces, Vet., Telegraph etc. etc.	1,741
Total for a, b, and c	42,137
Less carriers in (a) to (c) issued to Carbels	2,086
Total for (a) to (c) i therefore	40,051

(d)

East Africa Carrier Corps August to December 1914	3,576

(e)

Belgian Congo Carrier Corps ("Carbels")	8,429
Total (a) to (e)	52,056

(f)

"Job" porters for Belgian advance, "not organised", probably from Kigezi, short-term and short-distance	120,000

(g)

Mass levy 1917: fit for service out of 41,706	5,763
Grand Total (a) to (g)	177,819

(Lucas, 178,819; Watkins Report 183,003)

Wallis included the "Special Details" in the Carrier Section total of 40,051. He boosted Lucas' total by 1,000 with an extra 500 each for Uganda Pioneers and Belgian military telegraph construction, figures not mentioned in the Secretariat Minute.

Appendix

The Watkins Report (Appendix 1, Tables 1, 2 and 6) credits Uganda with 10,947 carriers for 1917-18, but only 5,763 could be raised for the mass levy. The 6,173 may have previously been with the Carrier Section and Carbels. There were no Uganda carriers on the books of the Military Labour Bureau until 1917.

Appendix 2

Pay, Food, and Equipment

1. Examples of Monthly Pay for African Followers

GRADE	MONTHLY PAY (with rations)
Interpreters	Rs.30
Cooks	Rs.25
Armed Scouts, 1st grade Transport drivers, House boys, Mountain Battery, Machine-Gun and Bomb Carriers, Stretcher Bearers, Signal Section, Hospital Dressers, Office Boys	Rs.10
1st grade Veterinary Dressers, Syces, herds, Ward Orderlies and Sweepers, Pier Gangs	Rs.12
Ammunition carriers (1st line Transport), Mail runners	Rs.10
Unskilled labour of all kinds subsequently	Rs.5 p.m. for 3 months Rs 6

(Indian and Swahili artisans were also paid by the Military Labour Bureau. An Indian carpenter might get over Rs. 100 a month with rations, a Swahili Rs.60).

Appendix

2. Improvements in Rations

31st December 1914: 1½ lbs flour (banana, mealie, *wimbi* or *mtama*), or rice for rice eaters. ¼ lb beans. ½ lb meat, or 1lb beans if meat is not available.
"Arabs, Swahili, Headmen to draw rations at scale for African Troops."
Train Rations: *29th February 1916:* 1 lb dates, 1/2 lb powa (per boiled rice).
22nd August 1917: 1/4 lb tinned meat, 1/2 lb biscuits instead of dates, 1/2 biscuits instead of powa.

17th October 1917: The same rations for all East African troops and followers. 8 oz fresh meat, 10 oz mealie meal, 10 oz rice, 4 oz beans 2 oz goor, 2 oz ghee or cooking oil, 1/2 oz salt, 6oz vegetables (potatoes, onions, sweet potatoes, *mhogo* or bananas), one piece soap, 2 oz tobacco weekly. If anything was not available, substitutes were ordered: date instead of rice, coconuts instead of oils, beans, ghee and goor instead of fresh meat. If troops could not cook in the field, 1/2 lb preserved meat (or 1 lb dates or groundnuts) and 1 lb biscuits were to be substituted. *(Watkins Report, Appendix 3, Table 1, and MLB Handbook)*

3. Clothing and Equipment

	A	B	C	D	E	F	G	H
Blankets	1	1	1	1	1	1	1	1
Haversacks	1	1	1	1	1	1	1	1
Waterbottles	1	1	1	1	1	1	1	1
Identity discs & cord	1	1	1	1	1	1	1	1
Khaki shorts	1	1	-	1	1	1	1	1
Boots or sandals	1	1	-	1	1	1	-	1
Jumper	1	-	1	-	1	1	1	1
Jumper with shoulder pad	-	-	-	-	-	1	-	-
Putties (pairs)	-	1	-	1	1	1	1	1
Tarboosh and cover	-	-	-	1	1	1	-	1
Shirts (magari)	-	1	-	-	1	-	-	-
Khaki frocks	-	1	-	1	-	-	-	-
Warm coats (followers)	-	1	-	-	-	-	-	-

	A	B	C	D	E	F	G	H
Chevrons (NCO's stripes)	-	-	-	-	-	1	-	1
Medical brassard	1	-	-	-	-	1	-	-
Blanket straps	-	-	-	-	-	-	-	-

The Letters represent the following Grades:-

A. African followers and transport boys.
B. Transport headmen and Cape Boys.
C. Carriers.
D. Native Intelligence Agents.
E. Armed Scouts.
F. Gun Carriers, Stretcher Bearers and Signal Porters.
G. Africans of Telegraph Section.
H. Carrier Police.

The lowliest grades were A, G and C in about that order. Some of A and F would be medical personnel wearing brassards. G perhaps needed putties to protect their legs against rough telegraph poles. D, E, F and H are marked out for their higher military standing by their tarbooshes and putties; some would wear the chevrons of sergeants and corporals.

Appendix 3

Some Medical Statistics

A. The Uganda Transport Corps Carrier Section, a force of 32,896, suffered 1,557 deaths in 1915 and 1916:

1.	Dysentery and diarrhoea	338
2.	Cerebro-spinal meningitis	319
3.	Pneumonia and bronchitis	157
4.	Malaria	25
5.	Small pox	1
6.	Killed in action	7
7.	All others	79
8.	Unknown	331
9.	Missing, presumed dead	290
	Total	1,557
	Death rate	*4.73%*

The number missing was 434, of whom 290 (two thirds) were presumed dead. This includes no deaths before January 1915, either in Uganda or in the East Africa Protectorate, or in Carbels. Except during the advance on Tabora in 1916, these men would not have served very far from their homes, or probably for very long. (Source as for Appendix 1: NAU/SMP 4290.)

B. Deaths between April and November 1917 inclusive among porters from the East Africa Protectorate, Uganda and German East Africa, from the four diseases.

	April	May	June	July	Aug.	Nov.
1. Dysentery	500	590	1,315	1,170	940	400
2. Pneumonia	170	255	415	270	255	220
3. Malaria	75	115	390	280	210	140
4. Cerebro-Spinal Meningitis	45	55	85	145	105	65

The numbers in the field were at their highest: 105,898

The most severe operations were during October and November.

Select Bibliography and Sources

1. Documentary Sources

A: Official records

(i) Kenya National Archives

Seyidie Province 1914 to 1918.

16/49 files 1 and 2, Provincial and District Annual Reports

37/577, eleven files, "Porters for the Military."

38/579-643, civil and military labour.

43/914 - 46/1074, Carrier Corps and military situation in Taita, Nyika and Vanga.

DC/ITTA/1-3, war diary of DC Taita District.

Nyanza Province 1914-1918.

PC/NZA/1/10-13, Provincial Annual Reports. See also District Reports and *Political Record Books.*

Kenia and Ukamba Provinces 1914 to 1918.

PC/CP/1/1-9, Kenia and Ukamba Political Record Books, 1901-1926.

PC/CP4/1/1, Kenia Province Annual Reports, 1914-1921.

PC/CP4/2/1-2, Ukamba Province Annual Reports, 1906-1921.

DC/NYI/1/2, Nyeri District Annual Reports, 1903-1931.

DC/NYI/3/1 & 5, PC/2/1, Nyeri District Political Records.

DC/FH4/3, Fort Hall District Political Records 1912-1920.

DC/FH6/1, History of Fort Hall 1888-1944.

PC/CP6/3/1, "Emigration from Reserves 1917."

DC/MRU/1/1, Meru District Annual Reports, 1912-1924.

DC/EBU/3/2, Embu District Political Records, 1917-1958.

DC/KBU/1/5-14, Kiambu District and Dagoretti Sub-district Annual Reports, 1913-1921; DC/KBU/3/3-13 & 25, Political Records.

DC/MKS/1/1-6, Ukamba: Provincial and District Annual Reports.

DC/MKS/4/1-6, Machakos District Political Records 1911-1920.

Ukamba Inward 75/47, for the 1899 Caravan disaster.

(ii)   Central Government Library

"Report by Lieutenant-Colonel O.F. Watkins, C.B.E., D.S.O., Director of Military Labour to the B.E.A. Expeditionary Force, on the period from August 4th, 1914 to September 15th, 1919" - the Watkins Report, typescript, two copies.

Lieutenant-Colonel H.C.E. Barnes, Director of Military Audit, "Report on War Expenditure, British East Africa 1915-1917.

(iii)   University of Nairobi, Department of History, Research Project Archives

War F/1/2, Entebbe Secretariat Papers, especially NAU/SMP 4290, "Uganda Transport Corps, medical and statistical matters".

War F/1/3, Tanganyika National Archives, especially Secretariat Wi/19351, "Unclaimed Wages (in respect of War Service) due to Natives" with a copy of Kenya Government Despatch No. 83, February 1931: the history of the Porters' Claim.

This collection was made by Dr. Brian G. McIntosh; the author is deeply indebted to the History Department for access to this material, and acknowledges all quotations from its Archives.

(iv) Public Record Office, London

Colonial Office Records

CO 533, East Africa Protectorate, vols. 140-216; vol. 216 contains the full copy of the Watkins Report, with appendices.

CO 534, The King's African Rifles.

CO 536, Uganda, vols. 85, 86 and 88 for the recruitment question; vol. 90 for manpower statistics, and a copy of H.R. Wallis, *Handbook of Uganda*, 2nd edition

CO 544, *Executive and Legislative Council, E.A. protectorate.*

CO 822/34/26018, original copy of Despatch No. 83, with comments.

War Office

WO 106/46, "Scheme for operations against Germany East Africa, 1897."

Cabinet Papers

CAB 23/2, War Cabinet Minutes.

CAB 44/3-10. and CAB 45/6-74, materials for the unpublished Volume 2 of the Official History.

B. Private and Non-Official Records

(i) Rhodes House, Oxford

The Watkins Papers were made available to the author by Mrs. E.J.F. Knowles, daughter of O.F. Watkins, they were recently deposited at Rhodes House.

The Ainsworth Papers (Mss. Afr. 379-382) include his diary as Military Commissioner for Labour.

(ii)   Edinburgh University Library

The J/W. Arthur papers, for the Kikuyu Mission Volunteers.

(iii) The Royal Commonwealth Society Library

The H.B. Thomas papers are a small deposit of vital documents:

(a) the only known copy of the *Military Labour Bureau handbook.*

(b) a copy of Standing Orders and Regulations for the Forces in British East Africa, among other very interesting papers.

"The Reflections of Bishop Willis [of Uganda] 1872-1954" (typescript). [The R.C.S.L. is now part of the Cambridge University Library]

2. Published Sources

(A) Books

Armstrong, H.C., Grey Steel: J.C. Smuts, a study in Arrogance (London: Barker-Methuen, 1937).

Barra, G., 1,000 Kikuyu Proverbs (London: Macmillan, 1960).

Blixen, Karen, *Out of Africa* (London, Putnam, 1937).

Brett Young, Francis, *Marching on Tanga* (London: Collins, 1917).

Buchanan, Angus, *Three Years of War in East Africa* (London: John Murray, 1920).

Campbell, W.W., *East Africa by Motor Lorry* (London: John Murray, 1928).

Bibliography

Clayton, Anthony, and Donald D. Savage, *Government and Labour in Kenya 1895-1963* (London: Frank Cass, 1974).

Clifford, Hugh, *The Gold Coast Regiment in the East African Campaign* (London: John Murray, 1920).

Clyde, D.F., *History of the Medical Services of Tanganyika* (Dar es Salaam Government Press, 1962).

Cook, Albert, *Uganda Memories* (Kampala: Uganda Society, 1945).

Cranworth, Lord, *Kenya Chronicles* (London: Macmillan, 1919).

Delf, G., *Jomo Kenyatta* (London: Victor Gollanez, 1961).

Dolbey, R.V., *Sketches of the East Africa Campaign* (London: John Murray, 1918).

Downes, W.D., *With the Nigerians in German East Africa* (London: Methuen, 1919).

Dundas, C., *African Crossroads* (London: Macmillan, 1955).

Fendall, C.P., *The East African Force 1915-1919* (London: H.F. and G. Witherby, 1921).

Gardner, Brian, *German East; The Story of the First World War in East Africa* (London: Cassell, 1963).

Goldsmith, F.H., *John Ainsworth, Pioneer Kenyan Administrator 1864-1946* (London: Macmillan 1955).

Hancock, W.K., *Smuts: the Sanguine Years, 1870-1919* (Cambridge: Cambridge University Press, 1962).

Hill, M.F., *Permanent Way: The Story of the Kenya and Uganda Railway* (Nairobi: East African Railways and harbours, Second Edition, 1961).

_____. *Permanent Way Volume II: The Story of the Tanganyika*

Railways (Nairobi: East African Railways and Harbours, 1957).

Hobley, C.W., *Bantu Beliefs and Magic* (London: H.F. and G. Witherby, Second Edition, 19138).

_____. *Kenya from Chartered Company to Crown Colony* (London: Frank Cass, Second edition, 1970).

Hodges, Geoffrey, *The Carrier Corps: Military Labor in the East African Campaign, 1914-1918* (Westport, Connecticut: Greenwood Press, 1986).

_____. African Response to Europe's Rule in Kenya (to 1914) Hadith 3/Ed. B. Ogot EAPH 1971.

Hordern, Charles, *History of the Great War: Military Operations, East Africa, Vol. 1, August 1914 to September 1916* (London: His Majesty's Stationery Office, 1941).

Huxley, Elspeth, *Red Strangers* (London: Chatto and Windus, 1939).

Iliffe, John, *Tanganyika under German Rule 1905-1912* (London: Cambridge University Press, 1969).

Jones, W., *K.A.R.* (London: Arrowsmith, 1926).

Keane, G.J. and D.G. Tomblings, *The African Native Medical Corps in the East African Campaign* (London: Richard Clay and Sons, 1921).

Kenyatta J., *My People of Kikuyu* (Nairobi: Oxford University Press, 1966).

Lettow-Vorbeck, Paul von, *My Reminiscences of East Africa* (London: Hurst and Blackett, 1920).

Leys, Norman, *Kenya* (London, Frank Cass, Fourth Edition, 1973).

Bibliography

Lucas, Charles, *The Empire at War Vol. 4* (London: Oxford University Press, 1924).

Matson, A.T., *Nandi Resistance to British Rule 1890-1906*. vol. 1 (Nairobi: East African Publishing House, 1972).

Meinertzhagen, R., *Kenya Diary* (Edinburgh: Oliver and Boyd, 1960).

____. *Army Diary,* (Edinburgh, Oliver and Boyd, 1957).

Charles Miller, *Battle for the Bundu* (London: Mac Donald and Jane's, 1974).

Mitchell, Philip, *African Afterthoughts* (London: Hutchinson, 1954).

Mosley, Leonard, *Duel for Kilimanjaro* (London: Weidenfeld and Nicholson, 1963).

Moyse-Bartlett, H. *The King's African Riffles: A Study in the Military History of East and Central Africa, 1890-1945* (Aldershot: Gale and Polden, 1956).

Mungeam, G.H., *British Administration in Kenya 1895-1912* (Oxford: Clarendon Press, 1966).

Murray, S.S., *A Handbook of Nyasaland* (Zomba: Government Printer, 1922).

Philp, H.R.A., *God and the African in Kenya* (London: Marshall, Morgan and Scottland

____. *A New Day in Kenya* (London, World Dominion Press, 1936).

Reitz, D., *Trekking on* (London: Faber and Faber, 1933).

Rosberg, Carl G., and John Nottingham, *The Myth of "Mau Mau": Nationalism in Kenya* (Nairobi: East African Publishing House, 1966).

Roscoe, John, *The Baganda* (London: Macmillan, 1911).

Smith, H. Maynard, *Frank, Bishop of Zanzibar* (London: Society for the propagation of Christian Knowledge, 1926).

Thomas, H.B., *The Nile Quest: Speke Centenary Celebrations 1962* (Kampala: East African Literature Bureau, 1962).

Thuku, Harry, with Kenneth King, *An Autobiography* (Nairobi: Oxford University Press, 1970).

von Lettow, See Lettow-Vorbeck, Paul von.

Watkins E. Oscar From Africa - The Biography of Oscar Ferris Watkins 1877-1943 Radcliffe Press 1995.

Were, Gideon, S., *A History of the Abaluyia of Western Kenya* (Nairobi: East African Publishing House, 1967).

Weston, Frank, *The Black Slaves of Prussia* (Zanzibar: Universities' Mission to Central African, 1917).

____. *The Serfs of Great Britain* (London: Universities' Mission to Central Africa).

Wilson, C.J., *The Story of the East African Mounted Rifles* (Nairobi: East African Standard, 1938).

(B) Periodicals

Newspapers and magazines

Central Africa (Universities' Mission to Central Africa, London)

The East African Standard (Nairobi)

Inland Africa (African Inland Mission)

Kikuyu News (Church of Scotland, Kikuyu)

The Leader of British East Africa (Nairobi)

Journal Articles

Journal of African History

Hodges, G.W.T., "*African Manpower Statistics for the British Forces in East Africa, 1914-1918,*" 19,1 (1978).

Killingray, David, "*Repercussions of World War I on the Gold Coast,*" 19,1 (1978).

Ogot, Bethwell A., "*British Administration in the Central Nyanza District of Kenya, 1900-60*", 4, 2 (1963).

Page, Melvin E., "*The War of Thangata: Nyasaland and the East Africa Campaign, 1914-1918,*" 19.1 (1978).

Pirouet, M. Louise, "*East African Christians and World War I,*" 19,1 (1978).

Savage, Donald C., and J. Forbes Munro "*Carrier Corps Recruitment in the British East Africa protectorate 1914-1918,*" 7,2 (1966).

Hadith (Proceedings of the 1969 and 1970 conferences of the Historical Association of Kenya).

Hodges, G.W.T., *African Responses to European Rule in Kenya (to 1914).*

Journal of Hygiene

Kauntze, W.H., "*A Polyvalent Vaccine in the Treatment of Bacillary Dysentery in East Africa,*" (Part 1 of MD Thesis), 18, 4 (1920).

Kenya Medical Journal

Kauntze, W.H., "*A Polyvalent Vaccine in the Treatment of Bacillary Dysentery in East Africa,*" (Part 2 of MD Thesis), 3, 12 (1926-7).

Wilson, C.J., *Introducing a discussion on "Native Diets" at a meeting of the Kenya Branch of the British Medical Association*, 2, 5 (1925).

_____. *"Native Diets: a Lesson from Rhodesia,"* 2, 12 (1926).

Rhodes-Livingstone Journal

Shepperson, George, *"The Military History of British Central Africa,"* 26 (1960): review of H. Moyse-Bartlett, The King's African Rifles," (Aldershot, 1956).

Tanganyika Notes and Records

Taute, M., *"Medical Treatment on the German Side,"* 8 (1939).

3. Oral Sources

This is a complete record of all interviews carried out during 1969 and 1970, with the names of all witnesses, and of all the friends who supplied notes, arranged interviews, interpreted, translated tapes and simply accompanied the author on so many enjoyable journeys. He owes them a very great debt of gratitude for all their kindness and enthusiasm.

(A) Nyanza Province

(i)   Central Nyanza District : Bunyala

Raphael Simigini Osodo, 75 years old chief's clerk, 4 July 1970; Felix Osodo, his grandson, and Fred Ojiambo conducted the interview; Felix also provided notes.

Asembo Odera, 80 years old and Odandayo Mukhenye Agweli, 72 years old both askari in (Uganda) KAR, notes given by Felix Osodo.

Uyoma

Jonathan Okwirri, 86 years old, Senior Chief, Superior headman in Carrier Corps: his grandson Aloysius Ongutu conducted the interviews on 4 and 5 July 1970, assisted by Fred Ojiambo.

(ii) South Nyanza District:

Suna

Daniel Orenda, 93 years old, carrier; Nguka Nyaoke, 85 years old, carrier and stretcher bearer, notes given by Moses Oyugi.

Kisii

Otochi Onduko, age grade *Nyong'atita,* ammunition carrier, notes given by John Makori.

Homa Bay

Yohana Ojwang', 69 years old, carrier; Lazaro Maende, 72 years, carrier; William Adiang, 70 years, KAR askari, notes given by Vitalis Ojode.

Oketch Atonga, 78 years, machine gun carrier, notes given by Richard Siaga, 26 August 1970.

(B) Rift Valley Province

Thomson's Falls

Macharia Gacuca, 70 years old, houseboy; Wanjira Gichuhi, 80 years; Kang'au Mugambi, 90 years; the first two were from Nyeri; notes given by James Kuruga.

(C) Kenia Province

Meru District: Nyambene Division, Akithii Location

M'Laibuni wa Baikwamba, 80 years old, KAR askari; M'Kong'u wa M'Maitai, 85 years, Northern Frontier district carrier; M'Nkuraru wa M'Twamwari, age unknown, KAR askari; notes given by Zakayo Munene, 5,6 and 12 September, 1969.

M'Inoti wa Tirikimu, 75 year, postal carrier (Kajiado-Longido road) and Muthanya wa Muiri, over 75 years, KAR askari, both Kaaria age grade; notes given by Gervase Mutua.

Nyeri District: Mihoti, South Tetu

Kamau Kagimbi, askari, *Njaramba* age grade, 1913; Elijah Kaara, clerk at Nairobi Carrier Depot, later storeman, *Mbauni* (Pound) or *Mbia* (Rats) age grade 1914; notes given by Njagi Gakunju. The interview with Kaara was conducted by Njagi and James Kuruga, 7 November 1970.

Muranga (Fort Hall) District: Kabati Market

Gitombo Muri, cook; Ng'ethe Kamau, a driver; Mwaura Ng'ang'a. KAR askari; Wabunya Kahindo, who escaped the levy; all of *Njaranga* age grade; the interview was conducted by Njagi Gakunju and John Dick Waihenya, with Albert Muthee and Lawrence Narains.

Maragwa

James Beuttah. Telegraphist and political leader, interview 21 February 1970, in English.

Kirongo

Kihara Wahagi and wa Ngoto, both KMV; James Gatune and

Geoffrey Maina conducted the interview on 21 February 1970.

Kahuhia Church

Silas Kiige and Domenico, both *Murigi* age grade: Canon Nathaniel Gachina, *Kihiu Muiri* age grade; Ishmaeli, *Makanga* age grade; Samwel Ngoci, *Njaramba* age grade, all KMV; John Dick Waihenya and James Kuruga conducted the interview on 29 May 1970.

D: Ukamba Province

Kiambu District: Limuru area

Marius Ng'ang'a Karatu, 85, ox-cart driver and hospital dresser, later political activist; Kinyanjui wa Mukura, 84, *Nyarigi* age grade, carrier, and Nathaniel Mahingu, about 85, KMV; the interviews were conducted by Kinyanjui's son Peter in June 1969.

Joseph Mundia, *Mbauni* age grade, cook; Leah Nyamuiru Karuga, *Ndungu* age grade; these interviews and further talks with Marius Karatu and Kinyanjui wa Mukura, were conducted by Ngure Mwaniki (Leah's grandson), Njagi Gakunju, Danson Mukuria Kimani and Geoffrey Maina on 8 November 1969; between them they translated the tapes from both sets of interviews.

Ngecha

Kinuthia, *Kamande* age grade; Gachuguma wa Kanyoko, *Kanyutu* age grade; Kaniaru, *Kihiu Muiri* age grade; Kangethe wa Nyaruchi, all Kikuyu Mission Volunteers; also a KAR askari, *Kihiu Muiri* age grade, name omitted; the interview was conducted on 10 May 1970, and the tapes translated by Luciano Njonjo and Njagi Gakunju.

Kabete

Josphat Muranga Njoroge, KMV, *Kihiu Muiri* age grade, notes given by Danson Mukuria Kimani.

Ngugi, machine-gun carrier, *Kihiu Muiri* age grade, notes given by Lawrence Gitau.

Josiah Njonjo, DC's clerk, later Senior Chief, interview at Kibichiku Farm, in English on 12 November 1970.

Machakos District: Muthetheni

Umoa Mbatha, about 85 years old, carrier headman, and Muasya Maitha, 90 years, ammunition carrier; Nguku Mulwa, 85 years, syce and mule driver; two interviews conducted by Raphael Thyaka, on 14 June 1969; tapes translated by Philip Mwalali and Ezekiel Musau.

Nzioki Wambua, 80 years, KAR askari, notes given by R. Thyaka.

Kiu

William Kwinga Nthenge, 85, stretcher bearer, and Mwova Kataka, 85, KMV; the interview was conducted by Fred Katule and John Mang'oka, December 1969; Fred also gave notes.

Kimumo Kitui, 81, stretcher bearer, later KAR askari; Kavai Longe, 75, askari; notes given by Fred Katule.

Kilungu

Musembi Kiindu, 80, ammunition carrier, and Muindu Kathuli, carrier and mule driver; Ezekiel Musau conducted the interview on 3 October 1970, assisted by Philip Mwalali.

Mulovi Kivandi, 86, excused from service; the interview was

conducted on 3 October 1970 by his grandson Ezekiel Musau, assisted by Philip Mwalali.

Mbwika Kivandi, 83, KAR askari, brother of Mulovi, notes on both given by Ezekiel Musau.

Kiteta

Mulei Nguyo, 85, KAR askari and storekeeper; Mutiso Kanzivei, 90, carrier; Muindi Ngaui, 86, carrier headman; notes given by Philip Mwalali.

Mukaa

Muumbi Mulei, 81 years old, messenger and mobile clinic orderly; Silvano Mutiso Mwoloi, 73 years, medical orderly; Nduma Muti, 79 years, carrier headman; notes given by John Mang'oka.

The author is much indebted to Dr. J. Forbes Munro of Glasgow University, for the following notes:

Iveti: Joseph Muinde, askari; Makau Nzibu, carrier.

Kilungu: Moses Kyele, carrier.

Kangundu: Kosiah Munyaka Kivangule, KMV, retired AIM pastor.

Machakos: Joseph Munyao, clerk.

E: Seyidie Province

Kaloleni, Giriama

Mwanyula Bikatana, over 90 years old, ammunition carrier with the German forces; the interview was conducted by Matthias Mwagonah and Christopher Katana (his great-nephew) on 26 January 1970; the tape was translated by Simeon Mkalla and Crispin Yongo.

Note: A better method for interviewing proved to be for the interpreters to provide a running translation. Closer attention could then be paid to the evidence as it was given. No subsequent translation was needed. The author emphasises his gratitude to all who helped with the oral work, as witnesses, companions or translators, for their inestimable contribution to this book.

Index

African labour, 4
African Memorandum, 202
African Native Medical Corps, 129, 139
African soldiers, 84, 109
African war experiences, 106, 108, 109, 145, 146, 187
African welfare, 151
Agweli, Odandayo Mukhenya, 107, 179, 192, 207
Ainsworth, John, 3, 11, 22, 25, 44, 129, 132, 138, 151
  recruitment of labour, 98, 101
Aitken, Major-General, 31
Alliance High School, 209
Anderson, Captain Thomas, 195
Animal transport, 51, 53, 70, 72
Arab Rifles, 21, 63
Arab ruling class, 76
Army Divisions, 81, 84
Arthur, Rev. Dr. John W., 112, 135, 138
Asian conscription, 36, 73
Askari Kanga, 204
Atonga, Okech, 42, 47, 179, 193, 205
Atrocity stories, 113
Austria, 33
Awards, 37, 194
Bagamoyo, 84
Baganda carriers, 47
Baikwamba, M'Laibuni wa, 191

Bananas, 124, 153
Barlow, A.R., 12, 136, 202
Basudde, Daudi, 203
Battle of Mahiwa, 101
Beans, 152
Beasts of burden, 70
Beazley, Colonel, 55
Beer, 151, 162
Belfield, Sir Henry, 30, 72
Belgian Congo, 16
Belgians, 88, 104, 189
Beri-beri, 151
Berlin Act, 23, 29
Best, Jack, 209
Beuttah, James, 197, 203, 208
Bikatana, Mwanyula, 10
Bishop of Zanzibar, 112, 113
Bismarck, 23
Blixen, Karen, 36
Boer War, 29
Bolomatari, 189
Bombay Light Infantry, 25
Boredom, 186
Bowring, C.C., 137, 139
British imperial forces, 15
British missionaries, 112
Buchanan, Angus, 55
Buganda Agreement, 130
Bukoba, 88
Buxton, Miss, 127

Byatt, Horace, 97
Cameroons, 2, 29
Cannibalism, 188
Caravan
    porters, 6
    routes, 8
Carnelly, Captain J.H., 163
    reports and letters, 166, 169
Carpenter, G.H. Hale, 47
Carrier Corps, xii, 1, 3, 13, 211
    depots, 14
    duties, 17, 88
    expansion, 81
    formation, 14, 31
    recruitment, 17, 35, 36, 211, 213
    registration of, 107
    status, 69
Carrier Depot Officers, 176
Carrier officers, 163
    reminiscences, 164, 165, 167, 169
Carrier units, 112, 124, 136
Carrier welfare, 150
Carriers, 163
    administration, 163
    casualties, 92
    loads, 47, 48
    logistics, 47
    Nyasaland, 24
    pay accounts, 178
    paymasters, 179
    payments, 174, 176, 177, 179
    payrolls, 176
    reminiscences, 107, 108, 109
Casuals, 35, 100
Central Committee of Supply, 125, 154

Central Nyanza, 87, 197
Central Railway, 82, 124
Central Railway, 88
Chief Native Commissioner, 191
Chiefs, 196, 202, 207
Chiefs, colonial, 38
Chilembwe, John, 58
Chogoria Hospital, 147
Church Missionary Society, 112, 135
Church of Scotland, 135
Churchill, Winston, 181
Chwa, Daudi, 129
Circumcision, female, 148
Civilisations, 4
Clerk, 199
Clive Irvine, 147
Clothing, 193, 217
Coast Column Carriers, 120
Coast porters, 153
Coconuts, 157
Colonies, neutrality, 24, 29
Colonisation, 5
Colour bar, 209
Committee of Imperial Defence, 28
Compensation, 180
    British payments, 182
    German payments, 182
    next of kin, 181
    religious beliefs, 181
    unpaid wages, 181, 182, 184
Congo, 15, 88
Conscription, 36
    forceful, 44, 45, 47
    of Asians, 73

Index

of Europeans, 73
punitive, 38, 44
universal, 73
Convoy system, 49
Cotton growing, 130, 132
Cowardice, 187
Crown Colony of Kenya, 197
Currency, 202
Dagoretti Memorandum, 202, 204
Dancing, 190
Dar es Salaam, 84
Deaths, 220
   registers, 177
Decoys, 196
Defence plans, 28, 29, 31
Delamere, Lord, 39
Desertions, 70, 176, 177
Deventer, General van, 100, 133, 164
Devonshire Declaration, 209
Diarrhoea, 204
Diarrhoea, 138, 153
Diets, 124, 151, 153, 156, 162
Digo carriers, 67
Director of Military Labour, 177
Discharged carriers, 176, 177
   expenditure of earnings, 179, 181
Discipline, 190, 191, 194
Diseases, 91, 119, 126, 130, 138, 154, 162, 220
District Commissioners, 175
Dodoma-Iringa Line, 138, 147
Dogs, 147
Downes, Captain, 92

Dowry price, 147
Dressing, 194
Drought, 21
Drought's Skin Corps, 63
Dumping-System, 49
Dundas, Charles, 46
Duruma, 41, 138
Dysentery, 25, 119, 125, 128, 129, 138, 141, 153, 157, 160, 162, 204
East Africa Pay Corps, 175
East Africa Protectorate, 17, 26, 29, 33, 196
   military labour force, 17
   recruitment statistics, 211, 213
East African Campaign, 19, 22
East African Carrier Corps, 17, 67, 173
   formation, 64
East African Force, 59
East African Mounted Rifles, 58
East African Transport Carrier, 67
East African War Relief Fund, 47, 209
Educational services, 209
Edwards, Brigadier-General W.F.S., 159
Effects of the War, 186
Egypt, 97
Elkington, James Major, 11
English, 197
Equality, racial, 187
Equipment, 216
Ethnic interactions, 190
European farmers, 163

European military officers, 26
European war experiences, 187
Evangelism, 144, 147, 209
Ex-servicemen, 204, 206, 209
　insubodination, 208
Experiences, 186
Famine, 25, 108, 204
　of the maize bags, 41
Fazan, S.H., 208
Fendall, C.P. Brigadier-General, 68, 84, 165, 190
Finger Print Section, 178
Flogging, 170, 171, 192
Followers, 34
Followers, 34, 216
　recruitment, 36
Fontaine, S.H. La, 30, 59
Food
　carriers, 48
　inspection, 159
　preparation, 156, 158
　stuffs, 153
Footbal,l 190
France, 34
Ganda, 124
Gatherimu, Kinyanjui wa, 42, 137, 202
Gender roles, 7
German colonies, 2
German East Africa, 3
German forces, 60, 62
　retreat of, 104
German Schutztruppe, 1, 27
Germany, 33
Giriama, 41, 46
　rising, 41

Girouard, Sir Percy, 29
Gold Coast, 26
Gold Coast Regiment, 97
Gospel Missionary Society, 135
Graham, Lieut-Colonel, 30, 31
Gratuities, 202
Grogan, Major Ewart, 72, 88, 202
Hall, Francis, 25
Handeni road, 116, 117
Headmen, 38, 42
Headstraps, 7, 8
Health precautions, 191
Heroism, 1
Hill, Major Ernest, 155, 158
Hobley, Charles W., 25, 29, 174, 186
Homer, 1
Homesickness, 189
Hooper, Rev. H.D., 137, 138
Hoskins, Colonel A.R., 30
Hoskins, General, 95, 97, 99
Hunting safaris, 10
Hut tax, 202
Huxley, Elspeth, 43, 45
Ibo carriers, 170
Identification system, 167, 178, 200
Imperial British East Africa Company, 15
Indian Government, 26, 31, 33
Indian government, 23
　defense of British Colonies, 24
　expeditionary forces, 33
Indian troops, 24, 26, 32, 78
　infantry, 165

Indian troops, 88
Influenza, 138, 162, 204
Inspector-General of
    Communications, 159
Intelligence service, 30
Iringa, 89, 139, 140
Ishmaeli, 147
Jackson, Sir Frederick, 125
Jasin disaster, 61
Jiggers, 187
Jubaland, 27
Kaara, Elijah, 9, 38, 199, 203
Kabaka of Buganda, 129
Kagwa, Sir Apolo, 129
Kahuhia, 135
Kaiser, William II, 23
Kamandu, 174
Kamba, 7, 151, 153
    porters, 25
    soldiers, 42
Kang'ethe, Joseph, 197
Kanzivei, Mutiso, 41, 157, 189
Karanja, Philip, 197
Karatu, Marius Ng'ang'a, 71, 86, 162, 191, 198, 199
Kariakoo, 14
Kariakor, xii
    market, 14
    meaning, 15
Karuga, Leah, 42
Kataka, Mwova, 47, 145
Kavirondo Taxpayers' Association, 204
Kenia Province, 34
Kenya National Archives, 34

Kenyatta, Jomo, 197, 203
Keya, 108
Keya famine, 204
Kiambu, 197
Kiarie, chief, 37
Kihindo, Wabunya wa, 44
Kiige, Silas, 136, 147
Kiindu, Musembi, 188, 195
Kikuyu Central Association, 197, 203
Kikuyu Hospital, 136
Kikuyu Mission Volunteers, 54, 100, 112, 179, 197
    evangelism, 145, 147
    recruitment, 135, 138
    reminiscences, 145
    roots of conflicts, 140, 145, 148
Kikuyu Mission Volunteers, 139, 140
Kikuyu, 35, 39, 135, 147, 151, 153
    porters, 25
    women, 7
Kilindini Docks, 36
Kilwa, 85
Kilwa Kisiwani, 91
King's African Rifles, 1, 26
    effectiveness, 31
    expansion, 80, 85
Kinyanjui, chief, 37, 207
Kipande system, 167, 178, 200, 202, 203
Kipling, Rudyard, 109
Kisii 41, 45
Kitchener, Lord, 27, 28

Kitui, Kimumo, 106, 162, 195
Kivandi, Mbwika, 179, 190, 193
Kivanguli, Josiah Munyaka, 140
Kome, Kinga, 180
Konigsberg, 62
Kruger, President, 23
Kungu, Waruhiu wa, 197
Labour
    compulsory, 4, 36
    conditions, 11, 37
    demands, 36, 41
    forced, 4
    management, 15, 19, 191
    recruitment, 97
    recruitment, 101
    supply, 36
    unskilled, 36
    voluntary, 36
Lake steamers, 188
Land alienation, 203
Land Settlement Commission, 202
Leave scheme, 46
Leisure activities, 190
Lettow-Vorbeck, Colonel (later General) Paul von, 14, 28, 33, 80
    long march, 102
    military skills, 102
    military stores, 86
    retreat, 81, 104
Leys, Norman, 11, 37, 150
Lindi, 85, 138
    force, 96
Lines of communication, 51, 52, 59
Literacy, 196
Livestock, 39

Livingstone, David, 113
Long marches, 106, 109
Longe, Kavai, 205
Luo, 35, 153
Lyon, Major W.R., 163, 168
    carrier administration, 169, 170, 172, 174
    reports and letters, 169, 170, 172
Maasai, 137
Madness, 196
Maende, Lazaro, 108, 157, 196
Magadi Soda Company, 36
Mahingu, Nathaniel, 135, 137, 138, 143, 145, 200, 203
Mahiwa, Battle of, 100
Maitai, M'Kongo wa, 49
Maitha, Muasya, 108, 179
Maize, 125, 151
Maji Maji rebellion, 24
"Makorogothi" [Gold Coasters], 188
Malaria, 138, 141, 160
Malashi, 176
Malawi, 16
Manning, Sir William, 29
Marching songs, 47
Mass levy, 35, 81, 97, 99, 100, 104, 135
Mathangani, Wambugu wa, 38
Matoke, 124
Maxted, Captain, 191
Mayanja, Nasanairi, 180
Mazeras, 137
Mazrui clan, 76

Index

Mbagathi Barracks, 162
Mbatha, Umoa, 108, 162, 179
Mbiu, Koinange wa, 197, 199, 202
McClue, H.R., 74
Medals, 37, 193
Medical
  services, 150, 151, 208
  statistics, 219
Medicines, 150
Mehugu, Gitahi, 43
Meinertzhagen, Richard, 8, 21, 27, 109
Mendi porters, 171
Mengo Hospital, 128, 162
Meningitis, 119, 129
Mesopotamia, 31
Mikindani, 85
Military
  atrocities, 77
  conscription, 36
  operations, 64
  options, 33
  police, 26
  railways, 70, 177
  technology, 187
  transport corps, 173
Military Commissioner for Labour, 44, 99
Military Labour Bureau, 17, 78, 104, 177
Military Labour Bureau Handbook, 169, 172
Military Labour Bureau Handbook, 208
Military Labour Corps, 15, 18, 54, 106, 208
Military Labour Pay Ordinance, 180

Millet, 151
Milner, Lord, 181
Mines, 32
Missions, 209
  recruits, 113, 116
  schools, 136
  volunteers, 136
Mitchell, Sir Philip, 186
Mjanji Depot, 132
Mombasa Depot, 190
Montgomery, H.R., 205
Morris Carter Land Commission, 183
Mosquitoes, 138
Mountaineers, 7
Muhanga, 141
Muiri, Muthanya wa, 86
Mukura, Kinyanjui wa, 146, 162, 189, 200
Mulei, Mumbi, 192, 204
Mulwa, Nguku, 72, 157, 205
Mumia, 207
Mundia, Joseph, 199
Munyao, Joseph, 41
Murang'a, 197
Musanji, Prince Joseph, 129
Muslim civilization, 5
Muslim traders, 6
Mutahi, Wahome, 43
Mutie, Nduma, 192
Mutiny, 26
Mwanza, 88
Mwenya, Joseph, 183
Nairobi Carrier Depot, 104, 177

Nairobi Carrier Hospital, 160
Namibia, 2
Nandi Scouts, 38, 63
Native Affairs Department, 12
Native Authority Ordinance, 37
Native Followers Recruitment Ordinance, 35, 41, 72, 176
Native Labour Circular, 206
Native Labour Commission, 11, 150
Native Trust Fund Ordinance, 181
Naval
  power, 85
  supremacy, 61
Neutrality doctrine, 24, 29
Ngoci, Samwel, 136, 143, 147
Nguyo, Mulei, 44, 157, 162
Nigeria Carrier Corps, 163, 172
Nigerian Brigade, 55, 91, 96, 168
Nigerians, 189
Njonjo, Chief Josiah, 196, 208
Njoroge, Josphat, 10, 43, 147
Nominal rolls, 176
Norforce carriers, 104
Northcote, G.A.S., 46, 200
Northern Frontier District, 27
Northern Rhodesia, 16
Northey, Brigadier-General (later Sir) Edward, 76, 89, 202
Nthenge, William, 47, 87, 157
Nubians, 192
Nyamwezi, 6, 39
Nyanza Province, 38
  porters from, 153
Nyanza Province, 34, 99

Nyanza, North, 204
Nyaoke, Nguka, 86, 179, 205
Nyasaland Field Force, 52, 89, 104
Nyasaland, 16, 26, 29
  carriers, 34
Nyika porters, 25
Nzibu, Makau, 156
Odera, Asembo, 45, 47, 107, 179, 204, 207
Ofwani, Orowa, 175
Ojwang, Yohana, 119
Okwirri, Jonathan (later Senior Chief), 35, 86, 189, 194, 197, 203
Onduko, Otochi, 158, 205
Onduso, chief, 36
Osborne, G.H., 180
Osodo, Raphael, 44, 47, 199, 207
Owen, Archdeacon, 204
Pangani, 84
Panyako, 208
Pasha, Emin, 27
Pay cards, 178
Pegasus, HMS, 62
Philp, H.R.A., 11, 38. 150
Pioneer Corps, 208
Pneumonia, 119
Pokomo, 41
Political developments, 196
Political systems, 9
Poll tax, 202
Porters' War, 2, 99, 100
Porters, 34, 89
  claim, 182
  claims, 181, 183

Index

front line, 106
loads, 49
long distance, 8
special, 35
Portuguese East Africa, 97
Post-war developments, 196
Post-war famine, 204
Posts, 49
Preparation for war, 70
Pretorius, 21
Promotions, 59, 193
Protest marches, 167
Protest movements, 197
Provincial records, 34
Public Works Department, 36
Punishment, 192, 194
Quinine, 77
Race Course Road Camp, 177
Racial
  equality, 209
  superiority, 188
Railway
  construction, 70
  extensions, 208
Rations, 55, 150, 156, 158, 165, 166, 217, 218
Reitz, Deneys, 91
Rejection rates, 134
Rejects, 167
Reminiscences, 108, 109, 145, 189
Repatriation, 46
Rhodes, Cecil, 23
Rhodesian mines, 208
Rice, 153, 158
Rift Valley farms, 36

Road construction, 63, 70
Road transport, 92
Rommel, Field Marshal Erwin, 13
Ruanda-Urundi occupation, 88
Rufiji, 91, 92
Rupee, 8, 202
Russia, 33
Safu, Nubi bin, 174
Said, Seyyid, 6
Salim, Bakari bin, 176
Salim, Sheikh Ali bin, 39
Sanitary problems, 126, 128, 153
Say, Mr. John, 172
Scott, Dr. Ralph, 106
Scott, Major E.L., 152, 191
Seaborne forces, 85
Selous, 21
Settlers, 35, 58
  power, 200
Seychellese stevedores, 159
Seyidie Province, 34, 39
Shilling, 202
Ships, 188
Sim sim, 157
Singing, 145, 190
Sireless stations, 28
Skin Corps, 21, 88
Slave trade, 6
Smallpox, 25, 138, 160
Smith-Dorrien, Sir Horace, 77
Smuts, General Jan, 77, 78, 81
  capture of territory, 86
  drive to Rufiji, 91
  handing over, 96

imperial War Cabinet, 96
  obsession with von Lettow-Vorbeck, 91
  war propaganda, 96
Snuff, 179
Soga, 124
  porters, 25
Soldier settlements, 202
Somaliland, 26
South African Horse, 164
South Africans, 73, 77
  troops, 77, 164
South-West Africa, 2, 29
Sowera, Lance-Corporal, 195
Spicer-Simson, 21
Spotted fever, 129
Squatters, 36
Sudanese, 192
Sugar cane, 158
Sultan of Zanzibar, 6
Survivors, 86
Swahili, 197
  caravans, 6
  language, 190
Sweet potatoes, 153
Tagi, 137, 138, 144
Tait, H.R., 136, 206
Taita porters, 25
Tanga 31, 32, 84
Tanga-Moshi railway, 81
Tanganyika, 2
Tate, H.R., 177
Taxes, 203
Taxes, 9, 176, 179
Technology, new, 187

Tenga-tenga, 89
Tetanus, 138
Thangata, 89
Thesiger, Colonel, 30
Thomas, H.B., 47, 130, 134
Thuku, Harry, 197, 199, 202, 203
Tighe, Major-General, 60
Tirikamu, M'Inoti wa, 108, 152
Togoland, 2
Trade routes, 5
Trade,
  internal, 6
  ivory, 5
  routes, 6
Transport
  animals, 86
  long distance, 5
  systems, 24
Transport Corps, 67
Transport systems, 26
Tribal police, 204
Tributes, 195
Troops, 26
Tsetse fly, 71
Turkana, 27
Uganda, 26
  carriers, 124, 130, 162
  diet, 124, 126, 128
  recruitment statistics, 213
  rejection rate, 134
  Eastern Province, 101
  military labour force, 16
Uganda Carrier Corps, 152
Uganda Native Medical Corps, 129
Uganda Railway, 6, 24, 36, 69
  defence of, 59, 60

Index

Uganda Rifles, 25
Uganda Stretcher Bearers Company, 128
Ukamba Province, 34
Universities' Mission to Central Africa, 112
Uyoma, 198
Vaccination, 162
Veterans, 27
Veterinary practice, 158
Voi, 24
Von Lettow-Vorbeck see Lettow-Vorbeck, Paul von, 86
Wages, 173, 176
  employment, 9
  unclaimed, 181
  unclaimed, 208
  unpaid, 182
Wagogo, 147
Wallis, H.R., 130, 133, 134
Wambua, Nzioki, 157, 205
Wambugu, chief, 37, 38, 163
Wapshare, Major General, 59, 71
War
  experiences, 107, 109, 187
  fronts, 59
  memorials, 1, 14, 195
  plans, 33
  songs, 190
  strategy, 23
War Council, 35, 73
Water supplies, 117

Watkins Report, 106
Watkins, Oscar Ferris, 12, 22, 64, 67, 69, 74, 130, 133, 177
Wavell, 21
Weather conditions, 91, 92, 167, 169
Welfare issues, 208
West African carriers, 97, 188
West African Force, 168
West African Frontier Force, 1, 26
West African troops, 91
Weston, Bishop Frank, 87, 112, 113, 115, 119, 121, 124
  discipline, 123
  recruitment of carriers, 113, 115
  reports and letters, 115, 117
Wilderness experience, 106
Wilson, Dr. C.J., 151, 153
Wimbi, 125
Working conditions, 13, 19
Young Buganda Association, 203
Young Kavirondo Association, 198, 203
Young Kikuyu Association, 203
Young, Francis Brett, 87, 187
Zambia, 16
Zanzibar Carrier Corps, 32, 112, 113, 116, 117, 120, 121, 123, 183
Zulu War, 77

www.ingramcontent.com/pod-product-compliance
Lightning Source LLC
Chambersburg PA
CBHW072138290426
44111CB00012B/1908